WHY CRAWL...
WHEN YOU CAN FLY?

RUTH AMPIAH-KWOFI

Grosvenor House
Publishing Limited

All rights reserved
Copyright © Ruth Ampiah-Kwofi, 2023

The right of Ruth Ampiah-Kwofi to be identified as the author of this
work has been asserted in accordance with Section 78
of the Copyright, Designs and Patents Act 1988

The book cover is copyright to Ruth Ampiah-Kwofi
Cover design copyright to Mary Melrose

This book is published by
Grosvenor House Publishing Ltd
Link House
140 The Broadway, Tolworth, Surrey, KT6 7HT.
www.grosvenorhousepublishing.co.uk

This book is sold subject to the conditions that it shall not, by way of
trade or otherwise, be lent, resold, hired out or otherwise circulated
without the author's or publisher's prior consent in any form of
binding or cover other than that in which it is published and
without a similar condition including this condition being
imposed on the subsequent purchaser.

A CIP record for this book
is available from the British Library

ISBN 978-1-80381-551-0
eBook ISBN 978-1-80381-552-7

DEDICATION

This book is dedicated to everyone who helped me on my journey of transformation.

To Paul and Jo Naughton who saw what I couldn't see in me. Thank you not just for seeing, but also for helping to bring it out.

To my daughters, Carlien and Amy. Thank you for being the precious gifts that you are in my life, thank you for grabbing hold of Jesus with both hands and never letting go. You know that you make me the proudest mama on this earth.

To my dear siblings, I know we have always been a unit, but thank you for sticking with me through thick and thin and for always believing in me.

To God, the Father, the Potter, who painstakingly reformed me into a vessel He could use.

Thank you from the bottom of my heart.

FOREWORD

Why Crawl When You Can Fly is a must-read for anyone who wants to fulfill their destiny. You will laugh, you will cry, and you will see yourself in its pages. Ruth unpacks powerful Biblical truths which are interwoven with great personal honesty. As you read, you will better understand yourself and you will discover how to be free from the hidden issues that have been holding you back. This is a book you will want to come back to again and again.

Pastor Jo Naughton, Whole Heart Ministries

This is way more than a book! The wisdom of years, decades of ministry behind the scenes in serving great men and women of God, and the "slings and arrows of outrageous fortune" as Shakespeare coined it, have been distilled into a wonderful manual for living. Its pearls of wisdom are packed with experience that money can't buy. The Bible says "buy wisdom and do not sell it". Great advice when buying this book. It will truly bless you.

Pastor Paul Naughton, Senior Pastor,
Harvest Church London

This book is a collection of great anecdotes gleaned from the author's personal life and a remarkable depth of knowledge of the Bible. It is an amazing gem that belongs in everyone's Christian library. Ruth confronts us with the raw, naked, and often painful truths of life, and gives us tried, tested and efficacious answers from the Bible, to the riddles of life. Her faith shines through all her tests, and this wonderful book provides many words of wisdom for all situations and complexities of life. This book is excellent in providing practical steps every reader can easily follow to move from just crawling in life to find freedom in flying, which is what God always planned for each of us. I highly recommend this book to you.

Rev Robert Ampiah-Kwofi, General Overseer,
Global Revival Ministries

PREFACE

"The zigzags of your life are but a straight line to God".

I wrote this book to bring hope to anyone who feels their life hasn't quite gone according to plan. To bring hope to those who have been discouraged by delays, disappointments and setbacks. To those who feel weighed down by life's events and feel like their life is going nowhere, like the only thing changing in their life is their age.

Whatever the zigzags have been, I want to tell you that destiny still calls. Our lives can often appear messy, just like the underside of a woven rug, but once you turn the rug over you see a beautiful pattern.

All through the ups and downs in our lives, God is weaving his plan, a beautiful picture called your destiny.

I pray that you will be truly blessed as you join me on the journey of transformation from a caterpillar into a beautiful butterfly.

CONTENTS

PART ONE-CRAWLING ALONG   1
  We Come As We Are   3
  I Didn't Know Whom I had Believed   9
  Lord, I Want To Want To   27
  Face-to-Face with Truth   39

PART TWO-GROWING PAINS   81
  Getting Rid of our Excess Baggage   83
  Pride Stinks to God   87
  The Prison of Unforgiveness   103
  Offence – The Blessing Blocker   115
  Lack of Honour   129

PART THREE-BECOMING IS NOT FOR QUITTERS   145
  The Remaking   147
  Don't Waste Your Pain   161
  Process – God's Quality Control Mechanism   173
  Becoming Fit for Purpose   199

PART FOUR-EMERGING UNRECOGNISABLE   209
  Reformed   211
  Putting on Humility   229

PART FIVE-FLYING FREE   249
  Conformed to His Image   251

'God told Jeremiah, "Up on your feet! Go to the potter's house. When you get there, I'll tell you what I have to say." So I went to the potter's house, and sure enough, the potter was there, working away at his wheel. Whenever the pot the potter was working on turned out badly, as sometimes happens when you are working with clay, the potter would simply start over and use the same clay to make another pot.'

Jeremiah 18: 1-4 (MSG).

God is the Potter and we are the clay. The Potter has a vision of how He wants each of us to turn out. When He sees that the vessel is not turning out the way He envisioned, He starts over and uses the same clay to make another pot. The Potter simply reforms the vessel using the same clay.

PART ONE
Crawling along

WE COME AS WE ARE

(then the Potter gets to work)

We come as we are

The caterpillar starts life short and stubby with no wings at all. It couldn't fly even if it wanted to. It's a wonder that a seemingly unattractive, inconspicuous creature can undergo such a dramatic transformation to become a new creature of such beauty and grace.

At the right time, the caterpillar forms a hardened outer protective layer called a chrysalis. When we look from the outside, the caterpillar looks like it is just resting, and nothing is happening. But inside the chrysalis is where all of the action is, the caterpillar is changing rapidly. Its internal makeup is undergoing a remarkable process called metamorphosis. It is this process that transforms this short, stubby creature into a beautiful and majestic butterfly.

By the time the metamorphosis is complete, everything about the caterpillar has changed. Its tissue, limbs and organs have all been changed. To become a beautiful butterfly, the caterpillar has to fall apart completely. In fact, it literally dies in order to live. There is nothing left of it. Metamorphosis has taken place and now the butterfly is ready to emerge. The caterpillar has become a butterfly. It is completely unrecognisable, a new creature, reformed and ready to fly. It has become the best version of itself, bringing life and joy to its environment.

This is a beautiful picture of what our Lord, the Potter, seeks to do with each of us. The Potter has the blueprint for your life and once we give Him the go-ahead, He then gets to work. He works any impurities out of the clay and works into us the things that belong. He goes to work shaping, moulding and firing so that we can emerge as a butterfly and not remain a caterpillar.

God's objective for each of us is that we fulfil all of our potential and become the person that He created us to be. His plan is always for us to fly and not crawl.

Jeremiah 29:11 (NIV) says, "'For I know the plans I have for you," declares the Lord, "plans to prosper you and not to harm you, plans to give you hope and a future.'"

Lord Send Me

Was it a tug on your heart? Perhaps a silent desire for more in your walk with God because you realised that there just had to be more. You wanted to do more than just go to church and be a good Christian. Maybe you've always wanted to make a difference to others, and become a force for change.

But then there were the questions. What? How? Where? What would it entail? What do I have to give up? Do I even have what it takes? What if it doesn't work out? How do I get to make a difference in the Kingdom? Where would the resources come from? Would God even want to use me?

There were more questions than answers, so you ignored the tug and got on with life. But that dream or desire didn't go away. Instead, every now and then there's that tug on your heart again. It's quite possible you never even shared it with your closest friend. Who knows, maybe you never voiced it out loud. Or you just wrote it in your journal and called it wishful thinking.

Lord my dream is to open a home for teenage mums.

Lord, I want to work with children who have been abused.

Lord, I want to be able to love as you do.

Lord, I wish I could reach out to people in prison and tell them there is hope.

Lord, I wish I could lay hands on people and see them get healed.

And finally, you gave in to that tug and, perhaps with some trepidation, you said, Lord, use me in your kingdom. Lord, send me. These were the words of the prophet Isaiah in Is 6:8 (NKJV) when he heard the voice of the Lord saying, "'Whom shall I send? And who will go for Us?' Isaiah replied, 'Here am I. Send me!'"

God always hears your heart. He hears those silent prayers and He answers that silent desire of your heart, that tug to be more, to do more and to touch the lives of others. Isaiah 65:24 (NIV) puts it like this: 'Before they call, I will answer; while they are still speaking, I will hear.'

He was the one doing the tugging all along. The Potter was tugging at your heart waiting for the go-ahead so that He could begin His work. Somewhere in our journey of walking with God, we start to desire more of Him. We desire to be useful in His Kingdom. We want to transition from being a child to becoming a son or daughter. This is because we are made in His image and according to His likeness as stated in Genesis 1:26-27 (NKJV): 'Then God said, "Let Us make man in Our image, according to Our likeness … So God created man in His own image; in the image of God He created him; male and female He created them.' We were created to be the best version of ourselves.

"Lord, send me" is actually an invitation to the Potter that says, "Lord, make me". The purpose of the making is so that we can look like Him, because we are made in His image and likeness.

We come as we are but there needs to be a reforming before we can become the best version of ourselves. Every butterfly you see started out life as a caterpillar.

The Potter begins…

I DIDN'T KNOW WHOM I HAD BELIEVED

2 Timothy 1:12 AMP: 'For I know Him [and I am personally acquainted with Him] whom I have believed [with absolute trust and confidence in Him and in the truth of His deity], and I am persuaded [beyond any doubt].'

Believing In a Stranger

Can we be in a real meaningful relationship with someone we do not know? Would we be able to trust that person? Would we be able to truly commit our heart to them?

If you've ever been in love then you know the excitement and the anticipation you felt anytime you were going to see that person. You loved their voice, their quirks, and their smile just made your heart melt. You made it a point to know their favourite movie and what foods they loved or hated. You loved spending time with them and hanging out together.

Apostle Paul made an intriguing statement in 2 Timothy 1:12 (AMP) when he wrote: 'This is why I suffer as I do. Still, I am not ashamed; for I know Him [and I am personally acquainted with Him] whom I have believed [with absolute trust and confidence in Him and in the truth of His deity], and I am persuaded [beyond any doubt] that He is able to guard that which I have entrusted to Him until that day [when I stand before Him].' After Paul believed in Jesus, he says he became personally acquainted with Him and that brought him to the point of being convinced about who the person he had believed in really was. He then goes on to say that because he knew Him, he trusted Him and therefore he was persuaded beyond any doubt.

Paul clearly knew things about Jesus which made him able to endure untold challenges without fear or complaint. What was it he knew and how did he get to know it? What is it that pastors, men and women of God know about Jesus that makes them so confident of results when they pray for the sick or preach the word or prophesy? Why is it that when we or someone in our lives needs healing, we also ask our pastors to pray even though we have prayed already? Do they have an inside line to God that we don't have? Maybe it's because we don't really believe our own prayers. There is a conviction that only comes from personally knowing whom we have believed.

When our father in the faith, Abraham, first encountered God, he was an idol worshipper but as he continued to walk with God, he became known as the father of faith. Romans 4:18-22 (NKJV) gives us the reasons why Abraham is called the father of faith. It tells us that he hoped against hope, that, despite his age, his wife Sarah's age and her barrenness, he believed what God told him about being a father of many nations. Verse 21 reads, 'And being fully convinced that what He had promised He was also able to perform.' In short, Abraham knew whom he had believed.

We need to come to the place of being fully convinced. We start off by believing and receiving Christ into our hearts but we must embark on getting to know Him personally, otherwise we will struggle with our convictions. We need to know Him in His integrity and also in His ability. Who is this person I have believed? Is He trustworthy? Can He help me? Is He willing to help me? We each have to come to the place where we can answer these questions for ourselves.

The Bible is full of stories about God's exploits on behalf of His chosen people, about mighty miracles and signs and wonders He performed to deliver His people. The Bible also tells us about God's goodness and mercy towards us, that God is love and demonstrated His love by sending His only son, Jesus, to die on the cross for our sins. We can read about these truths but until we know the person behind the mighty exploits and the loving acts, we will continue to lack conviction and persuasion whenever our faith is challenged – and it will be. Our faith will be based on someone we know of but do not really know. We will lack the courage of our convictions; struggle to stand up for the truth and for what we believe in the face of ridicule. God invites us in James 4:8 to draw near to Him and He will draw near to us too.

Getting to know Jesus in my downstairs bathroom

It was the year 2000, a new millennium, a new decade and a new year. A milestone birthday was looming and I was very conscious that something was missing in my Christian walk. I didn't seem that different from my non-Christian friends. There were times I wanted to give it all up because I felt like I was a fake. I knew there had to be more to this Christian life than what I had experienced so far, and I was determined to find out what it was. One day I cried out and said, 'Lord, show me what these pastors know that I don't know about you or else on Sundays I might as well go to a car boot sale instead!' I added for good measure that I was not going to attend a conference to find out. I wanted Him to teach me Himself.

My younger daughter was three years old and had never slept through the night due to a skin condition. When she finally began to sleep through the night, I felt I could finally catch up on years of lost sleep. God, however, had other plans. I shared at my small group meeting that I felt God was calling me to pray more and spend more time with Him. However, every evening when I settled down to pray, I would promptly fall asleep. My small group leader suggested that I schedule my time alone with God for the early morning. Initially, I said no way – I'm catching up on three years of lost sleep! But all the ladies in our group encouraged me to give it a go. Some of them said they did that for a whole hour before going off to work or school runs. My first thoughts were what could you and God possibly have to say to each other that would need a whole hour but I eventually agreed to give it a go.

The first challenge was where the Lord and I would have our morning meetings. The girls were aged three and six and tended to follow me everywhere. I needed some privacy, so I settled on the downstairs bathroom, which was unusually large and so had enough room for me to pace up and down. Plus, I could use the bathroom seat for a chair if I needed to sit down. My initial thought was that it was a bit irreverent to meet with God in a bathroom, but I made peace with that and said, 'Lord, if you don't mind then this is where we will be meeting.' I set aside every weekday morning from 6:30 to 7:15 to spend time getting to know the Lord.

I wanted to move from thinking God was some distant being far away to experience the reality of His presence with me continually.

And right there, in that downstairs bathroom, began a glorious season of discovery for me of getting to know the One whom I had believed. A season of getting to know who He was and not just what He could do for me.

Find a place in your home, your secret place where you meet with Him to fellowship. You will find that most times, if not always, when you get there, He is already waiting for you. It is in the secret place that you start to become fully convinced about the person you have believed.

It's simply a relationship between a Father and His child

Quiet time, morning devotion, call it what you will. As Christians, we usually have a time that we set aside to read the Bible and pray to God. There are all sorts of devotionals out there to help us do this by providing a structure to follow; in fact, we are spoilt for choice as to which ones to use. I had a devotional I used for my quiet times but when I began intentionally meeting with God, those meetings ended up being a lot more unstructured; they became more of "a getting-to-know-someone session". I called it freestyle – simply because I didn't really know what to do and I wasn't going to use my daily devotional. If there was a protocol then I didn't know what it was. How do you start? Who do you address? God the Father? What about Jesus and what about the Holy Spirit? And do you say good morning? But what if it isn't morning in heaven? Are there mornings in heaven where they live? I decided you couldn't go wrong with greeting all three of them so I would say, 'Good Morning, dear Father, good morning, dear Lord Jesus, and good morning, dear Holy Spirit.'

OK, I've greeted them – what next? This scripture in Psalm 100:4-5 (NKJV) came to mind – 'Enter into His gates with thanksgiving and into His courts with praise. Be thankful to Him, and bless His name. For the Lord is good; His mercy is everlasting, And His truth endures to all generations.' I live in London and I have actually been to Buckingham Palace before, so I would picture myself walking to the fancy iron gates and giving God thanks as I walked through them. Then I would imagine myself crossing the huge courtyard and I would give Him praise as I kept approaching the front door on my way to meet with the King. The King of glory. And then, once I'm in, the awe of His presence would make me go quiet, at a loss for words, but I could so feel His presence and His love fill that bathroom that there was really no need for words. All I had to do was enjoy the moment and bask in His presence, in the silence of true fellowship. Sometimes I would read a psalm to Him because, despite being talkative, I would often run out of words to say. As I spent quality time with Him, I went from wondering how anyone could possibly fill a whole hour alone with the Lord to wishing I could stay longer. I began to enjoy our times together so much that it was always a shame to have to stop after 45 minutes to go and get the girls ready for school and then go off to work.

The love affair begins in the secret place. David expressed in Psalm 42:1 (NKJV), 'As the deer pants for the water brooks, so pants my soul for you O God.' We are being awakened to the reality of this person we have believed. We have a desire to please Him, to spend time with Him and to communicate with Him. It's no longer something you have to do but rather something you want to do. It becomes worth giving up your sleep when you are excited about meeting with someone. I encourage you to create that secret place and you will not look back.

Changes

After a few weeks, I began to notice some changes. And then other people began to notice too.

I had a new understanding

The first change I noticed was that the Word of God suddenly came alive when I read it. Until then it had been a real struggle for me to understand the Bible. I would avoid Bible study meetings because I felt that what I understood was always different from everyone else. But now I could understand what many well-known scriptures really meant. It was like somebody was switching lights on in my mind. Many scriptures I knew began to come alive and make sense to me. The Lord would give me analogies about their meaning which clarified so much for me. His words were finally entering my inner man and so it was giving me light (revelation) and understanding. This is how it is expressed in Psalm 119:130 (NKJV): 'The entrance of Your words gives light; It gives understanding to the simple.' It is the Holy Spirit who quickens the Word of God to our spirits, otherwise, they are just words in a big book.

I had a conviction and boldness about my faith

I began to notice a new boldness when it came to my faith. Proverbs 28:1b (NKJV) puts it like this – 'But the righteous are bold as a lion.' I no longer felt slightly embarrassed to pray over my meal in a restaurant and I didn't think twice about sharing my faith when I had the opportunity. Once you are convinced, it becomes so much easier to convince others. It's very difficult to convince someone else about anything you are yourself unsure about.

I was becoming a better giver

I changed from being what I called a "yo-yo tither" to becoming a consistent tither. I changed from thinking I couldn't afford to tithe to knowing that I couldn't afford not to tithe because now I knew I could trust the Lord to stretch the 90% rather than try to depend on myself by holding on to the 100%. In Proverbs 11:24 (NKJV) we are told that, 'There is one who scatters, yet increases more; And there is one who withholds more than is right, but it leads to poverty.' Somehow, I could now trust God to be my provider instead of trying to hold on to everything that I earned.

I had more discernment

I began to grow in discernment. I would just know certain things, especially about people or situations. This is a great help, especially in the area of business. I would know the outcome of situations before they happened. My business partner, who is not a Christian, noticed it and would say, 'Ruth, you're on something - there's something different about you.' I would reply by saying I wasn't on anything, just spending more time with the Lord. Then he would say, 'Whatever you are doing, it's working, so keep doing it.'

How come these changes were only now happening when I had been a Christian for several years? What was I doing differently? Why was I suddenly changing so much? I realised that it was because I now had a secret place. I was getting to know whom I had believed and so now I could trust Him. You can never trust someone you do not know and you can never know someone without spending quality time with them regularly. It was a precious, precious journey of discovery for me. I came to what for many is a very obvious realisation. Christianity is nothing short of a relationship – a relationship between a Father and His child. I didn't recall anyone spelling it out in that way to me. It isn't a bunch of rules you do your best to keep and often fail at. No, a thousand times no! It is a relationship between your Father God and you. He ever lives in us through the Holy Spirit, who reveals more and more about Him to us as we fellowship together.

As you continue this journey, your faith becomes more and more real. You learn He is a real person and you actually want to please Him. You do not want to displease Him. You want Him to be happy whenever He looks at you. You become secure in the knowledge that the Creator of the universe is rooting for you. The knowledge moves from your head into your heart.

How well do you know your Father God? How much time do you give the Holy Spirit? How involved is He in your everyday life? He so wants to do life with you - teach you, guide you, laugh with you, cry with you, hold your hand when you need it. Will you give Him the time? Don't let busyness rob you of knowing whom you have believed. Don't let busyness rob you of true fellowship. Don't deceive yourself by allowing doing things for Him to replace spending time with Him. An exchange takes place as we remain in His presence, He takes our anxieties and gives us His peace, gives us joy in exchange for our sadness.

The book of Nehemiah 8:10 (NKJV) tells us, 'For the joy of the Lord is your strength'. And in Psalm 16:11 (NKJV), the psalmist declares, 'You will show me the path of life; In Your presence is fullness of joy; At Your right hand are pleasures forevermore.'

If the joy of the Lord is our strength and if fullness of joy comes from His presence, then not being in His presence regularly means our joy is depleted and no joy equals no strength. If pleasures evermore are at His right hand, then not being around Him regularly deprives us of great pleasure which cannot be found anywhere else. Let us endeavour to be in His presence as often as we can and savour every moment too.

Getting to know His voice

When you know someone well you know their voice. Jesus spoke these words to His disciples in John 10:27 (NKJV) – 'My sheep hear My voice, and I know them, and they follow Me.' Sheep respond to their shepherd. We serve a living God who speaks to us. In the constant noise and voices in our world trying to influence our choices and our responses, we need to be able to distinguish which is His voice, which is our own voice and which is the voice of the enemy. Knowing His voice means we can be guided by His superior knowledge and foreknowledge in every area of our lives – in our work, relationships, homes, health, and in our finances. Knowing His voice means we can be alerted to danger long before it rears its head. Knowing His voice means He can send us as answers to others in response to their prayers. Knowing His voice means we can walk in tandem with Him instead of running ahead or lagging behind Him. Knowing His voice means He can give us direction.

It was exciting to see the changes taking place in my life and I wanted to know Him more. One morning, in prayer, I said, 'Lord, I want to know your voice. You speak to others so please speak to me too.' When you pray, expect God to answer but don't define how the answer should come or you might miss it.

I would sit with Him in silence hoping to hear His voice but apart from a wonderful sense of His presence, I didn't hear anything. Eventually, I decided that if I heard what I thought was His voice, I would judge it by two things – is it a good thing to do and is it in the

Bible? If the answer was yes then I would go ahead and do it anyway because even if I was wrong, I would have done a good deed.

One evening, I had just cooked dinner and my husband was watching television. I heard a voice in my head say, why don't you serve him his dinner?

After ignoring the voice repeatedly, I stopped and thought, whose voice was that? It had to be the Lord's because the way I was feeling towards my husband at the time, there was no way I was going to suggest that to myself. Oh dear, I had asked the Lord to speak to me so I obeyed, rather reluctantly.

Another day, I walked into Primark, a popular department store, and passed by some clothes which had fallen on the floor. I heard a voice say, why don't you go back and pick them up. Since I didn't throw the clothes on the floor, again, I ignored the voice and kept walking. I heard the voice say again, why don't you go back and pick them up. I just knew it was the Lord speaking to me, so I turned around and went back to pick them up. I had asked to know His voice and now I couldn't pretend that He was not speaking to me.

God has such a sense of humour. There I was, expecting to hear a strong baritone voice telling me something I considered deeply spiritual. Instead, I was being told to be nice to someone getting on my last nerve and to pick up clothes from a shop floor when I didn't knock them over – that's our Lord for you. It's our obedience in the little things that He uses to mature us. He moulds our character as we learn to listen to and obey His voice. It is usually a still, small voice and easy to ignore, but we ignore His voice to our own detriment. God is always speaking to us. If we will stop to listen, we will always hear Him, encouraging, correcting and teaching us.

Have you been asking Him to speak to you? He will – keep obeying that voice and before long you will recognise His voice to you. It will always line up with His word.

First, we believe and receive Him into our lives, then we must begin to build a relationship with the one we have believed. Unless we invest in this relationship, our Christian walk remains a constant struggle and we are not very fruitful. The only way we get to know someone better is by spending time with them. As we get to know Him, we learn to recognise His voice, we become familiar with His ways and how He does things. As we begin to know His character, His integrity and also His ability we become persuaded that in every situation we can trust this person that we have believed. We begin to understand that we cannot bear any lasting fruit in our flesh and we become willing to die to ourselves so that He can live more and more through us. We can trust in the Lord with all our hearts and we stop leaning on our own understanding. Instead, in all our ways we acknowledge Him so that He can direct our paths just like it says in Proverbs 3:5-6 (NKJV).

Then we can join Apostle Paul in 2 Tim 1:12 (NKJV) to say, 'For I know whom I have believed and I am persuaded.'

Let us pray this together: *Lord, I want to grow closer to You, to know You more intimately. I choose to draw nearer to You by spending more time with You. I ask for the grace to diligently seek You because everyone who seeks finds. Give me a hunger for more of You, like the deer pants for water, let me pant after You until I can also confidently say that I know whom I have believed.*

In Jesus name, Amen

'LORD, I WANT TO WANT TO'

Philippians 2:13 (NKJV): 'For it is God who works in you both to will and to do for His good pleasure.'

Gaining desire – 'Lord, give me my want to'

I wish I was one of those people who had a nice smooth journey of always loving the Lord and wanting to serve Him. Instead, I was in the category of those who loved the Lord but had absolutely no desire whatsoever to serve Him. My biggest fear used to be that God would ask me to become a missionary and send me to Timbuktu. Not that I knew anything about Timbuktu beyond the little I learnt in geography or that being a missionary is not a noble calling, but at the time I had this notion that serving God was only about hardship and giving up everything I loved. I decided that the only way to avoid Timbuktu was to never ask God to use me – just in case He asked me to go to a faraway country miles away from my family, creature comforts and everything familiar. I loved my life too much and I certainly had no intention of going out of my comfort zone or sacrificing the plans I had made for myself.

Desire can be spontaneous or it can grow gradually. Some of us had a great desire to serve God right from the moment we received Jesus into our hearts. We grabbed Him with both hands and never looked back. It was spontaneous. For others, however, we love the Lord and yet have absolutely no interest in translating that into active Kingdom service. It could be because we feel unqualified, unspiritual or just fearful, so we resolve to keep our heads down, be a good Christian and leave serving God to others.

In the Bible, we read about how God tends to use the unlikely and sometimes the unwilling to achieve His purposes. As the saying goes, God doesn't call the qualified, He qualifies the called. There is a call of God on each of our lives whether we recognise it or not. There is a call to ministry in different spheres of life and, for each of us, there is a place waiting for us whether it is in education, family or entertainment. God declares through the prophet in Jeremiah 29:11 (NIV), 'For I know the plans I have for you, plans to prosper you and not to harm you, plans to give you hope and a future.' He also tells us in Ephesians 3:20 that He is able to do exceedingly and abundantly above all that we ask or think. His plans for us are truly much bigger than we think. God does not allow us to stay in our comfort zone but rather He calls us to leave that zone and let Him take us into places so far beyond what we could ever imagine, that the only way we can function there is in His strength.

We may see ourselves as the practical one who helps out behind the scenes and never wants to be out in front and yet we may have a gift to preach! We could be busy working in the bookshop and never consider that we have been blessed with a ministry involving children. God may have put in us an anointing for business which we are completely unaware of. It is often the people around us who recognise these gifts and abilities in us that we do not see or believe we have. God will sometimes orchestrate situations that will push us out of whichever comfortable place we have carved for ourselves and place us in the arena that He plans for us to be in.

There is always a price to be paid in exchange for any kind of anointing. There are things we need to lay down as we choose to follow the unique path laid out for us. The path to destiny fulfilment will always take us outside our comfort zones because of the size of God's plan for us.

Step out of your comfort zone

A comfort zone can be described as that state in which things feel familiar to us. We are at ease and in control of our environment and not experiencing anxiety and stress.

When it comes to serving God, our comfort zone is the place where we are comfortable in what we are doing, it is convenient and in line with what *we* planned to do for Him. When God decides to ask us to come up higher, it can be very scary because it is invariably not what we planned, bigger than what we planned and we usually do not consider ourselves to be ready or qualified. In short, it's always something we cannot do without His help. While God is very specifically showing that He wants to use us, inadequacies and all, we are screaming, 'No, Lord, please use someone else!'

Whenever I was called upon to speak in church, I felt completely outside my comfort zone. I'd always felt like I was an oddball among other Christians and that my take on spiritual things didn't quite fit the mould. Feeling inadequate and different meant that I was always horrified whenever I would find my name down to share a short word on giving. There were many others who I knew would jump at the chance *and* do a superb job, surely Pastor ought to ask one of them? When I pointed this out to him, he replied, 'Go and ask the Holy Spirit.' Even I knew better than that, so I resigned myself to praying and asking the Lord for a word to share about giving. As I pressed on in prayer, I would always get hold of something to share. Each time I shared, it seemed to minister to people while all I could think about was how everyone could probably hear my heart beating loudly and my voice shaking with fear. I continued to do it whenever I was asked to, out of obedience to God and my pastor, but I never enjoyed it or looked forward to any part of it. I didn't like the fact that I felt so filled with fear and self-doubt or the fact that it wasn't something I found easy to do.

You may be finding yourself right where I was, nervous about speaking out or approaching people or singing despite your beautiful voice. There is a myriad of situations that cause us to feel we are outside our comfort zone and it is natural to want to stay in the place of comfort and ease. We may not be ready yet to lay things down, to step out in obedience even though we love the Lord wholeheartedly. "I'm scared", "I can't", "I might fail" are only a few of the things we say to avoid leaving our comfort zone. But are any of our excuses for staying in our comfort zones acceptable when God is calling us to come up higher?

Excuses

We come up with all kinds of excuses to remain in our comfort zone. When faced with a challenge, our minds can go into overdrive thinking about what excuse we can give in order to wriggle out of it. Do we acquire a sore throat, a prior appointment or a family urgency that only we can deal with? We don't think of them as lies (which they are) – we just see them as excuses. Excuses are the "legitimate" reasons we give for why we cannot do something we don't really want to do. Many of us have a bagful of excuses we pull out when it suits us.

My excuse was that since I took much longer than most people to prepare any message, I needed at least a month's notice before being asked to share anything. This worked for a while but every now and then a surprise would be "sprung" on me. Anytime I was asked to lead prayer or share the word without prior notice, fear would rear its head. Instead of welcoming the opportunity, I saw it all as someone trying to show me up and embarrass me. It was so not comfort zone stuff for me. It was all about me and how uncomfortable I felt. I never considered that perhaps the Lord had put something in my mouth to say that would bless others. It was much later on that I learnt that all I needed to do was yield to the Holy Spirit and do it in His ability and not mine.

Excuses, excuses, excuses – what's in your bag of excuses? What legitimate reasons do we give for running away from what God is calling us to do? I'm too short, too tall, too young, too old, I'm single, I'm married, I'm scared, I'm inadequate, I'm not good enough – I could go on but I'm sure you catch my drift. People have been using excuses to try and wriggle out of the call of God on their lives for centuries.

In Exodus 3 and 4, Moses' excuse was, 'Lord, who am I? Lord, I'm not eloquent, Lord send someone else.'

In Judges 6, Gideon's excuse was, 'Lord, my clan is the weakest in my tribe. Lord, I am the youngest in my family.'

Saul's excuse in 1 Samuel 9:21 was, 'My tribe is the smallest. My clan is the least in my tribe.'

We tell God what He already knows about us and we give Him the reasons why He is wrong in choosing us to do something. We do this because we think success depends on us when all He is asking us to do is to partner with Him. God has all the power, strength and resources needed for any undertaking. What He does need is a vessel that He can flow through and that is where we come in.

The day my pastor invited me to join her leadership team, I looked for every reason why I couldn't because the truth was, I simply did not want to. I didn't want to be a leader in the church. I didn't want to do something I felt I wasn't any good at. Why didn't she invite someone who would love to be part of her team? Plus, I found her rather too intense and passionate about God and that just wasn't my thing. All my excuses were swirling in my head and I started to wheel them out. I didn't know how to pray like the others, I didn't fit in and I wasn't cut out for this. I was a good church treasurer, which I truly believed to be my calling. I was very happy living in my comfort zone – why would I want to leave there? I still remember her saying to me, 'You don't have to be like anyone else – just be you.' That was very liberating for me. Finally, I asked her if she was sure that it was God who asked her to invite me into her group and she said absolutely yes. Well, you can't exactly say no to God, can you? We all know what happened to Jonah when he tried to wriggle out of his assignment. So there I was, obedient but still very unwilling. Serving God but rather reluctantly and somehow that didn't seem right. Everyone else seemed to be willing and thought it a great privilege while I saw it as a heavy chore, my "cross" that I had to bear.

Reluctant? Ask for desire

If you find that you don't have the desire for what God is asking you to do it is absolutely fine, just ask Him for it. God will work into our hearts the desire we need in order to do whatever He asks of us. Philippians 2:13 (NKJV) states, 'For it is God who works in you both to will and to do for His good pleasure.' Isn't it wonderful that God will even give us the willingness we may be missing? All we have to do is just ask Him for it.

This is exactly what happened to me as I continued to minister when I was asked to. There was never a single day when I did it out of desire, it was always out of obedience. Then one day I thought, *Why don't you ask God to give you the desire for what He is asking you to do?* Obedience is great but wouldn't it be even better if we could have desire in addition to obedience?

I prayed a simple prayer: *Lord, I want to want to because right now I don't want to. Lord, please give me the "want to" so that I can look forward to sharing or preaching rather than dreading it.* I must have prayed like this for over a year while still doing the dreaded offering talks and the odd preaching here and there while giving my excuses whenever I could. One day, as

I was stepping up onto the podium to give an offering talk, I realised that the awful sinking feeling in my stomach wasn't there and the butterflies had gone. I thought, *Wow, He gave me the "want to" at last.* Desire to serve Him came to my heart and dispelled all my reluctance.

Along the way, I've learnt that it's only hard when you try to do it in your own strength. The load is only heavy when you try to carry it by yourself. Once you surrender all to Him, you find that His yoke really is easy and His burden really is light.

I want you to be encouraged because it is absolutely okay if, at first, you don't have the desire to serve God in any capacity. You may not have the "want to" even though you sense the call of God or your leaders see the call of God on your life. Don't keep making excuses because it's outside your comfort zone but just do it anyway in obedience. This is your sacrifice to God and while you continue to do it in obedience, keep asking for the "want to". I've got bag loads of it now simply because I asked for it. To God be the glory.

If like me you are looking for your "want to" then join me as we pray: *Lord, I love You and I do want to obey*

Your call to come up higher. Thank You for the privilege of wanting to use me. I surrender my fears, my feelings of inadequacy and whatever else I have used as an excuse to not step into Your call on my life. Today I ask You to give me the desire for the things that You are calling me into. Give me what it takes to desire what You desire for me to do. I thank You in advance for giving me desire. In Jesus name I pray, Amen

FACE-TO-FACE WITH TRUTH (Ouch!)

Truth is the starting place

'What is your name?' the Lord asked Jacob in his wrestling encounter with the angel in Genesis 32:27(NKJV).

'Jacob,' he answered.

What's in a name? Our identity. It's what we are known as and known by. Jacob's name meant trickster and he had pretty much been living up to his name until then. Just as He did with Jacob, the Lord will take us through a season where He starts off with the same question. When the Lord asks us a question, it is not for information but rather to make a point, to draw our attention to something. When Jacob finally faced the truth about who he was, God then gave him a new name – a new identity.

Sometimes the truth hurts. It can hurt to hear negative feedback. It can hurt when your spouse points out a weakness of yours. Or your housemate highlights one of your off-putting habits. Once we come face-to-face with the truth, some character and mindset adjustments are usually required. The only way to properly kill a tree is to cut it down to its roots. Trees often have complex root systems which enable them to grow back as long as the roots remain, but when the roots die the tree will also die and, more importantly, it can never grow back again. Whenever the Holy Spirit wants to address something in our lives, He deals with it at the root and that requires facing the truth about it.

One of the names of the Holy Spirit is the Spirit of Truth. This was the name Jesus used in John 16:13 (NLT) when He said to the disciples, 'When the Spirit of truth comes, He will guide you into all truth. He will not speak on His own but will tell you what He has heard. He will tell you about the future.' The Holy Spirit is the one who brings conviction, highlights the areas in our lives that need to change and then works in us to bring about that change. The Spirit of Truth is the one who brings us face-to-face with the hidden things in our hearts, which, if left unchecked, will sabotage our destiny.

As the Potter embarks on the process of reforming, He will bring us face-to-face with the truth about ourselves. What has become marred in our lives? It may have become such an integral part of us that we may not even be aware of it. It could be anger, unforgiveness or a complaining attitude. It could be an entitlement mentality or a competitive attitude or a hardened heart.

So many landmines can lie hidden, waiting to destroy our destinies. Very often, God has to address our personal beliefs, doctrines, and attitudes that do not conform to His Word, and which stand in the way of us fulfilling our destinies in Christ, and we must be willing to submit to His will.

My own doctrine

It is easy to end up with attitudes, mindsets, and beliefs which we consider are compatible with our Christian walk, only to discover, as we grow in Him, that they are entirely alien to the culture of God's Kingdom.

Are you impressed by your gifts, skills, and abilities? Are you impressed by your achievements, position, job, or career? Or impressed by your brilliant personality and popularity? Do any of these make you quietly think to yourself, *How great I art*? Or do you shy away from anything that shines the light on you or involves standing out in any way? Maybe that's your definition of being humble and yet God might be the one putting you in front to use the gift he placed inside you.

We can be full of our own spirit, whether by being overly self-confident and full of ourselves or intensely shy and averse to anything that would put the spotlight on us. The saddest thing is that we have no idea that anything is wrong. We continue to believe we are pretty good Christians while we fall short of God's best for us.

An eye for an eye – if anyone crosses your path, you make sure they do not forget it in a hurry. If you dislike someone, you feel you owe it to them to make them aware of it so that they can also dislike you. You are a strong person who doesn't suffer fools gladly. No one is going to treat you like a doormat and walk all over you. Silly people should not be allowed to remain silly and it is your duty to rescue them from their silliness. People who make poor choices have themselves to blame and should suffer the consequences of their choices so that they do not repeat the same mistakes. Tithing is a good practice to follow unless money is very short that month, in which case, it's okay to skip God since He isn't broke and doesn't need the money. People who hear the gospel and do not receive Christ straight away obviously want to fry in hell and should be left to exercise their choice.

The above summed up my Christian "worldview". It took the challenges I went through to bring me face-to-face with the truth about myself and to realise that many of my "personal" doctrines actually did not align with the Word of God. I was impressed by the favour I always seemed to attract. I was impressed by my abilities and skills at work. I was even impressed by the variety of my tongues-speaking. It took my inability to fix what I was going through myself to show me that I wasn't all that. It took going from being overly confident to almost becoming a nervous wreck and unsure of myself to accept that I didn't always have it together. It took becoming forgetful at times or making errors at work for me to learn what it was like to not always get things right. It took not having enough money with no one to turn to but God for help, to learn to depend on Him at all times and not on myself for finances. It took a life-altering crisis to get me to face the truth and to view my life through His eyes and now I am forever grateful for that long season of challenge because of the outcome.

Our personal doctrines may be influenced by our personality, our nurture, our culture, etc., and they appear right to us. Proverbs 14:12 (NKJV) points out that, 'There is a way that seems right to a man, but its end is the way of death.' Our way may appear fair or justifiable or politically correct and yet be completely counter to the word of God. Our doctrines can result in hardness of our hearts towards others or produce a lack of compassion towards others. They can cause us to offer judgement when we should be offering mercy. These doctrines often make us poor ambassadors of the Kingdom we belong to. Our focus remains on self instead of on Him.

As you allow the Spirit of Truth to do His work in your heart, one by one, and gradually, you start to give up your own "doctrines", which are not in alignment with His word, and you adopt His doctrines instead. You begin to change until you can hardly recognise yourself. Your reactions and responses become more loving and less about maintaining your reputation. You recognise that proving your point becomes less and less important. As Joyce Meyer put it, 'Being right is highly overrated.'

God, in His infinite mercy, will often allow us to go through situations that will cause us to face the truth about ourselves, then challenge our wrong doctrines and bring a turnaround so that we can align with His truths. Our challenges may not look like the mercy of God while we are experiencing them, but it is the resulting fruit that shows what He was doing during that time.

You may be a Christian who truly loves Jesus and yet still have your own doctrines which are completely contrary to God's will and purposes. My doctrines were all rooted in "an eye for an eye" – in judgement and not in love. How could I represent a God who is love when I had no love? How would I show His compassion if I believed compassion was for wimps?

What is your personal doctrine? What beliefs and attitudes and thought patterns do you still hold and live by which don't match up with God's word? Thank God that He loves us too much to leave us with our wrong doctrines. Endure His pruning, and allow the pruning to result in a renewing of your mind and in more and more fruit. He truly loves us too much to leave us the way we are.

But it's true, isn't it?

Our words are seeds. Seeds always reproduce after their kind and we harvest much more than what we planted. Our words can build others up or tear others down. Words can encourage someone or leave them completely deflated. Words can inflict deep wounds or bring joy to someone. Once they are out of our mouths it is impossible to recapture them. We see this happen in the home, with our spouses and our children. We see it in the workplace as we make cutting remarks to cut people. More and more we see it on social media, people using words as deadly weapons to wound and destroy others.

The enemy capitalises on this and causes us to use our tongues and our words to bring about division, complaining, rebellion, gossiping, etc. We can always say we are sorry but we can never take back the words once they're out. Even though the wounds may heal, they leave scars that always remain. That's why we are warned in Proverbs 18:21 (NKJV), 'Death and life are in the power of the tongue, and those who love it will eat its fruit.' We are further warned in James 3:5-6 (NKJV), 'Even so the tongue is a little member and boasts great things. See how great a forest a little fire kindles! And the tongue is a fire, a world of iniquity. The tongue is so set among our members that it defiles the whole body, and sets on fire the course of nature; and it is set on fire by hell.'

Knowing this, let us endeavour to be especially mindful of the kind of seeds we are sowing into our own lives and the lives of others by watching our words.

Perhaps you've always had a way with words. Perhaps you're very funny and people seem to laugh at almost everything you say. Maybe you're very witty and come up with all kinds of catchy quips pretty effortlessly, often at someone else's expense. Or you could be what I call the "senior housemistress", always the one ready to bring about a correction in every situation.

I used to pride myself on my plain-speaking and grew up thinking that as long as something was true, it was okay to say it to the person. It never crossed my mind that while it may be true it could also be unkind and hurtful to hear. Or that while it may be true the person was not yet in a place to do anything with my so-called "truth". I would say my "truth" to them, see their expression change and then add, 'But it's true, isn't it?' I knew I had a way with words, that I was not afraid of people's faces and that I had favour with people, but this did not give me licence to speak carelessly to anyone on the basis that what I was saying was true. It was many years before I learned that I was not called to speak the truth but rather to speak the truth in love. The "in love" portion took years to cultivate and it is still something that I have to consciously work on to keep my words loving and helpful.

While some statements may be true, they can also be very hurtful so instead of diving straight in with whatever I want to say, I had to learn to always stop and listen out for the leading of the Holy Spirit. When we listen out for Him to guide us, we are able to speak the right words at the right time to someone and they, in turn, are able to receive it and, most importantly, act on it.

God has called me to speak the truth in love. I believe He has given me the gift of saying tough things to people without them getting offended. They usually say that they can hear the love in my voice and that's why they can receive it.

King Solomon, the wisest person that ever lived, tells us in Ecclesiastes 3:1,7 (NIV) that, 'There is a time for everything, and a season for every activity under the heavens: a time to tear and a time to mend, a time to be silent and a time to speak.' There is a time and a place to speak into a person's life. We only earn this right by investing sufficiently into a relationship with the person. This places them in a place where they are assured of our love and so can receive encouragement as well as any negative feedback, we may give them. Just speaking by itself doesn't necessarily mean that you have been heard by the hearer. Especially when it comes to correction, you haven't communicated unless you are being heard. Ephesians 4:29 (NLT) instructs us to let everything we say be good and helpful so that our words will be an encouragement to those who hear them. We are further told in Colossians 4:6 (ESV), 'Let your speech always be gracious, seasoned with salt, so that you may know how you ought to answer each person.'

This lesson is for those of us who see ourselves as correctors and fixers. Let us learn to stop ourselves and ask the Holy Spirit for guidance whenever we feel the urge to speak into anyone's life or if someone seeks our opinion. Stop and ask yourself - is what you are about to say helpful to the person? Is it kind? Will it build them up? Or is it just true? Ask the Holy Spirit when it is the right time to speak. This could mean waiting and saying nothing in the moment in order not to embarrass someone. It could mean never speaking when we are angry so that we do not say something we will later regret or not saying something just to prove a point. Love must be reflected in our choice of words, our tone and our timing when we speak. Love is broken down for us in 1 Corinthians 13: 4-8 (NIV) – 'Love is patient, love is kind. It does not envy, it does not boast, it is not proud. It does not dishonour others, it is not self-seeking, it is not easily angered, it keeps no record of wrongs. Love does not delight in evil but rejoices with the truth. It always protects, always trusts, always hopes, always perseveres. Love never fails.' Are your words kind or cutting? Are they helpful or harmful? Yes, it may be true but is it loving? Whatever truth we speak, the hearer must be able to hear the love behind our words. Let us always endeavour to speak words that build others up and not put them down. Our words must encourage not discourage. Whenever you speak, always allow love to be your guide and then sow your words.

Our software and defaults

Just as the caterpillar is born preloaded with everything needed for it to become a butterfly, we all come preloaded with everything we need to fulfil our purpose, We are born uniquely preloaded with certain natural tendencies, skills, and gifts, which will enable us to fulfil our purpose. The analogy the Lord gave me was my laptop and the software that came with it when I purchased it. It came preloaded with basic software including Microsoft Office. Perhaps your software is MS Excel because you love figures and precision, and you like order and things to be just so. Another person's software may be antivirus, so they will have an eye for spotting errors and things that are not right and be good at correcting things. Someone else's software could be Final Cut Pro and they would be very creative with graphics, design and visuals.

This is why we must always be content and not try to compete with others or try to be like anyone else because we do not have the same software. Imagine trying to do beautiful graphics using MS Excel, the outcome would be less than mediocre. Whenever we try to do anything we are not called to do, we always find it a struggle and we will never do it well either. For example, a pastor is equipped with the heart of a shepherd while an evangelist isn't because they are never in one place long enough to need a shepherd's heart to nurture the flock. If the evangelist tried to be a pastor, they would be doing it without the pastor software and would probably end up causing a lot of havoc to the flock!

Having different software also means that we each have certain defaults that are not helpful in fulfilling our purpose. Sitting right next to our strengths are our weaknesses. As we allow the Spirit of Truth to work on our character, these weaknesses start to drop off so that only the treasure remains.

You can be bold, charismatic and forthright on one hand, while on the other hand, you are often insensitive with your words, ungracious and unwilling to cut people any slack. Or you could be kind, caring, and always ready to lend a helping hand, and yet no good at saying no because you think that it is mean to say no. You may end up worn out and maybe burnt out because of your inability to say no. God's pruning and moulding are what He uses to help us get rid of the impurities and leave only the pure gold that is useful in the Kingdom.

In short, to fulfil our purpose we need to "lose" some of our defaults in order to become who God made us to be. The process can at times be very painful. A pruned rose bush never looks pretty. It looks bare, small, even forlorn, but come spring you see the reddish shoots emerging and the new growth coming forth bigger, better and stronger too. You get many more blooms than if it had not been pruned. We are far more fruitful after the pruning so we must learn to yield to His pruning. It's like medicine – it might not taste good but it certainly makes you better.

Push through the tests

Whatever you may be going through right now, God has already programmed the capacity software in you to endure the test. The capacity is already within you to not only handle it, but to prevail as well. James 1:2-4 (NIV) tells us to, 'Consider it pure joy, my brothers and sisters, whenever you face trials of many kinds, because you know that the testing of your faith produces perseverance. Let perseverance finish its work so that you may be mature and complete, not lacking anything.'

Our attitude towards the test is what determines the outcome, not the size of the test itself. Our tests prepare us for promotion. Our tests prepare us for greatness and we are not expected to give up when we are being tested. Proverbs 24:10 (NKJV) points out, 'if you faint in the day of adversity then your strength is small.' God uses our tests and trials to build endurance, perseverance, compassion and an even greater capacity to overcome.

Joseph's many tests prepared him for the palace in Egypt. God gave him two wonderful dreams and then his "nightmare" began. Joseph's dream did not include slavery, or Potiphar's house or wrongful imprisonment. Joseph was headed for the palace but it was via the prison.

David's many tests prepared him to be king of Israel. The prophet anointed him to be the next king of Israel and that was the onset of his "nightmare". David's route to the palace was via the cave of Adullam, as a fugitive fleeing from King Saul. They both experienced many years when it looked like God's promise was never going to come to pass. They could have given up on God and gone into a deep depression but, instead, they both chose their attitude in the trials. They chose to trust God and kept their eyes on their promise from God. Jeremiah 12:5 (NIV) observes that, 'If you have raced with men on foot and they have worn you out, then how can you compete with horses?' This talks about the ability to persevere in the face of contrary winds or negative circumstances.

You could be going through a season of pruning right now which feels very painful and unpleasant. Perhaps you prayed for God to bless you financially and use you to support Kingdom expansion and soon after that you got made redundant from your job or your business collapsed. Or maybe you know you are called to be a prophet and yet the first few times you stepped out and prophesied you were wrong and it was as if you didn't hear God correctly. God uses tough seasons to prune us for greater fruitfulness. We must learn to embrace rather than try to pray away such seasons. The pruning helps build strength in us so that our very lives can be a testimony that brings God glory.

Don't despise the seasons of testing and trial – if you keep the right perspective during the trial, you always emerge with an intimate knowledge of more of His many names and attributes. If the season of challenge was one of ill health you will emerge with an intimate knowledge of the Healer. If all you've ever had is the odd headache and flu for which you took a painkiller, let's face it, you don't really know Him as Jehovah Rapha – the Lord who heals. It takes coming out of a life-threatening illness to have an intimate knowledge of His name as your Healer.

Pain is better out than in

We often hear that big boys don't cry but Jesus wept, Apostle Paul wept, Joseph wept and David wept too. These strong men were not afraid to release their tears. While weeping seems to come easier for most women, we sometimes think that adults shouldn't cry unless it is because of a bereavement. We often apologise when we are overcome and burst into tears. Some see it as a sign of weakness and yet tears are a release mechanism which God gave to us for the precise purpose of releasing built up pain. We must allow ourselves to let out some of the pressure built up in our emotional pressure cooker through our tears. We must give ourselves permission to cry. To cry over lost loved ones, lost dreams, lost relationships, lost health, lost jobs, lost businesses, over disappointments and delays, over expectations not being met. Life delivers many painful events, sometimes they are prolonged and seem never-ending. When we push down pain until we can no longer feel, it may numb the pain but it also shuts down our ability to release some of that pain through our tears and our solution simply creates another problem for us.

Use the release mechanism

The truth is that we are all carrying some level of pain around with us as a result of our life experiences. Many times, as Christians, when we experience painful events, we like to brush ourselves off and say we're okay. Except we're not. We've simply pushed the pain down and buried it somewhere. It may be out of sight but it's still in there somewhere, affecting our perspective and also feeding our doubts and fears. Pain is always better out than in because pain builds up and it accumulates. Facing the truth involves admitting that we are hurting and that we have unresolved pain, which is building up like the air in a pressure cooker. We must use the release valve, find a safe place and release the tears because it really is better out than in. Find a safe place to cry – run the bath; there's plenty of water in it so add some more. The car is good as well. Go to a park. Or in the arms of a close friend. Let the tears out and then wash your face. Once you put your face back on, you can then carry on with life. What I have just described is just the releasing – it is a great help but it does not make things go away, nor does it deal with the root cause or bring you healing. There are times when we may also need to seek help in the form of both spiritual and professional counselling, when we face very challenging situations. Please make sure you seek every help available to allow you to come out the other side.

God has designed us to always need Him for the complete healing and removal of pain. It is God giving us free therapy and it is very effective for healing emotional pain. When we bring Him our pain, when we release it in His presence through our words and our tears, He in turn removes our pain and heals our hearts.

Book an appointment

There's one more thing that you absolutely must do. When I have some serious business to do with God, I book an appointment with Him. So, go on, book your appointment – choose a time when you know there will be no distractions, ideally when there is no one else around, no one to hear you rant or cry or both – and then, as it directs in Lamentations 2:19 (NKJV), 'Pour out your heart like water before the face of the Lord.'

Tell Him like a little child telling their Dad how mean someone has been to them in the playground. Don't go into "religious mode" – just tell it like it was. How they wouldn't play your game, only theirs. How they all laughed at you when you tripped and fell. How they teased you about your large nose and how that hurt. Describe to Him exactly how it made you feel. The ridicule, the embarrassment, the shame everything you can remember. And then allow the floodgates to open. Let out the pain and cry until there's no more crying left in you. And then watch how He comforts you as only He can because He truly is the only one who knows how to fix it. He alone knows precisely what you need that will comfort you, encourage you, and, above all, heal you of that hurt so that it doesn't remain and cause you further damage. The Bible talks about the balm of Gilead. Sit in His presence and ask Him to rub some of His balm on your heart because it hurts so much. And then wash your face, square your shoulders and carry on – you will be much lighter because you let out your pain by articulating it to Him and better still you will come out with healing from your pain and a fresh new perspective. Sometimes that's all that is required and you can move on. The more regularly we press the release valve in His presence the less pain we carry around with us.

Squatters in the house

Painful events and adverse circumstances can attract further enemy activity into our lives. Satan looks for entry points in our lives as opportunities for demonic oppression. Traumatic events, bereavement and loss, relationship breakdowns, accidents and times of vulnerability can serve as entry points for oppression by the enemy. Facing the truth can reveal that we need deliverance as part of our healing. We may be completely unaware of this as we go about our daily lives, but the Holy Spirit will allow no hiding place for them in any area of our lives. The Spirit of Truth leaves no stone unturned as He unearths and uproots everything that does not belong in our lives if we let Him.

The word "squatters" took on a particular significance for me when God used it to deliver me from a fear of demons and spiritual warfare, which I'd had for many years. That year, I started praying that God should explain to me about demons in a way that would address this fear once and for all. While in prayer sometime later, I heard one word – "squatters" – and I knew immediately that it was the answer to my prayer. I looked the word up in the dictionary and the definition was "illegal occupants of unused buildings". Squatters can even acquire squatters' rights if they stay in a place long enough, which can make it difficult to evict them unless you go to court. The more I thought about squatters, the clearer it became – demons are squatters, trespassers, illegal occupants trying to take up residence in places that do not belong to them. Squatters must be evicted and we have been given the authority to evict any demons we come across in the name of Jesus. We don't have to be scared of them, instead, we have to exercise our spiritual authority and evict them. Just in case you are fearful of spiritual warfare and demons and the like – don't be – just remember that they are just squatters, illegal occupants, and if we discern their presence there is only one thing to do – evict them because they are trespassing. We have the authority to use His name and Philippians 2:10 (NKJV) says, 'That at the name of Jesus every knee should bow, of those in heaven, and of those on earth, and of those under the earth.'

As I practised pouring out my heart before the Lord more regularly, I discovered another reason why the Lord invites us to pour out our hearts before Him. Sometimes the healing we need requires deliverance first because of the presence of squatters. During a particularly challenging week, I had spent a whole day feeling tearful without knowing exactly why. I brought it before the Lord the next morning so I could just pour out my heart and cry out any arrears of crying that I may have been carrying. I really poured out my heart, how I felt cheated by life, how I felt like Joseph, who obeyed Him and ended up in prison. I cried until I was totally spent from crying and then I just sat on my bed in complete silence. I had said everything I wanted to say. I had cried all my crying too. As I sat there in silence, I heard that word again – squatters. This time I knew exactly what that meant, so I said, out loud, 'Any illegal occupants in my life, in my body, in my mind, or wherever, I command you to leave right now in Jesus' name!'

Immediately I began to cough so I reached out for some tissues as I realised I was being delivered of something. A couple of times I heard myself scream; the deliverance must have continued for about 15 minutes until I was calm again. As I sat calmly on my bed, I knew that what I had just experienced was deliverance. I had once read about deliverance in a book by Derek Prince: They shall Expel Demons. Right there on my own, I had experienced profound deliverance from the effects of many negative experiences I had gone through. I didn't know I needed deliverance but because I had poured out my heart before Him, He in turn had done for me what I needed at the time.

When we face the truth of our pain and bring it before Him, God is ever ready to help us deal with it and root out any squatters who may have taken advantage of our vulnerable state to oppress us in any way. Learn the importance of pouring your heart out like water before Him – no holds barred so that the Great Physician can do what only He can do to fix what needs fixing. Our close friends and family can offer us a listening ear and their sympathy, our therapist will help us process the pain and come to terms with it so that we can get on with our lives but only our Father God knows the precise remedy and antidote for whatever is ailing us. Make Him your first port of call when things get tough. Never hesitate to bring your pain before Him and tell Him how you are feeling. Even if it's Him you're angry with, still tell Him. Once you've poured out and after He completes any related clear-out, just sit in His presence and wait while He pours in His healing balm.

Use the right password

The password for entering into God's presence is given to us in Psalm 100: 4 (MSG): 'Enter with the password: "Thank you".' When things are not going well in our lives, we tend to focus on what isn't working and often forget what has worked. We forget to say thank you. We focus our thoughts on the prayers that haven't been answered instead of remembering the ones that have been answered. We forget about all the things we do have, like good health, or family or a roof over our heads, etc., because we generally take those things for granted and, instead, we keep thinking about the things we don't have. It's all about us and about what is missing in our lives. We forget that the Bible instructs us, in 1 Thessalonians 5:18 (NKJV), 'In everything give thanks; for this is the will of God in Christ Jesus for you.'

Another truth we all have to face is that gratitude opens doors while murmuring and complaining keeps them tightly shut. If we were not prone to forget we wouldn't have been given this reminder to remember to remain thankful in all things. Gratitude is key because you won't get past the gate without the right password. We don't get to see the King when we are unthankful.

'Thank you, Lord,' I said, one morning, as I was getting ready for work. Then I heard Him say, 'For what?' I didn't have anything in particular in mind when I said it, I was just feeling grateful and voiced it aloud. When I stopped to actually consider what I was grateful for, I answered, 'For the girls.' Because I could never stop being amazed at how good God had been to me when it came to the children.

The next thing I heard was that I should break it down. I began to thank Him for all the different things about my children that I was thankful for. For the improvements in their health, that their schoolwork hadn't suffered despite the turmoil at home with the divorce, that they have such a great relationship with each other, for the musical gifts He has given them both. My gratitude began to rise higher and higher as I spelt out all the things He had done in their lives. As I broke it down, I realised how different things could have turned out but for the goodness and mercy of God. That old song came to mind – "Count your blessings, name them one by one and it will surprise you what the Lord has done". I was so glad He asked me to break it down. My heart filled with gratitude to Him and faith for the future. When we acknowledge and verbalise how good He has been to us we are reminded of His faithfulness and then we have the faith to know that the God who changes not will also certainly take care of all the things that we are still believing Him for.

Take it a step further. What about all the things He does for us that we do not even know about? We say thank you for the things we do know about but there are countless things He does for us daily that we haven't got a clue about. The car accident that didn't happen because you got delayed at work? The embarrassment that didn't happen because He nudged you and said don't say anything and you obeyed. The exam you passed when we both know you should have failed.

Let's remember to say thank you for the things that He stopped from happening. Let's remember to thank Him for all the things we take for granted. I once heard a famous preacher say that she always thanked God for her kidneys working properly whenever she used the bathroom because she could be on dialysis. I thought she sounded a bit extreme and I laughed at what she said but as I began to understand the importance of gratitude, I realised that I too must be grateful for all the things I take for granted. The fact that I have good health. That I can walk and I'm not in a wheelchair. That I have a roof over my head.

When things are going well, we don't usually need to look too hard for things to be thankful for, but we still must not take God's goodness for granted. Instead, we must direct our appreciation to the source of all good things in our lives. When things are not going so well, we must be very intentional about our gratitude. On your worst day, look for something to be thankful for and then break it down into specifics, into the seemingly smallest or mundane things. As you appreciate God for His goodness, your perspective on your circumstances begins to change because your eyes are not focused on them but rather on God, the solution-provider. Why do I have to be grateful even when life is tough? Because the Bible gives us the key in Psalm 100:4 (NKJV): 'Enter into His gates with thanksgiving, And into His courts with praise. Be thankful to Him, and bless His name.' We enter His gates with thanksgiving. The entry password is "thank you". This means that I won't get past His gates without the correct password.

Remember remember

If gratitude gets me through the door, then it means that complaining and murmuring don't get me anywhere. All they do is cause doors to remain shut before me because I am using the wrong password. Lack of gratitude breeds an unattractive sense of entitlement which looks bad before God and before man. A lack of gratitude displeases God. This truth is easy to ignore and is responsible for the lengthening of our journey in the wilderness. We read in the book of Exodus about the Israelites in the wilderness. A journey of 11 days took 40 years and one of the main reasons was that they majored on complaining despite all the miracles God did for them. They saw God perform at least 10 miracles before they even left Egypt. Throughout the plagues, they lived in Goshen and were untouched by any of them. After that, they experienced the miracle of the parting of the Red Sea. They ate miracle food called manna, they drank water from a rock. Their clothes and shoes never wore out. And yet, at the appearance of any negative situation, they immediately forgot the mighty exploits of their God and complained and murmured instead. Their ingratitude was regularly on display and was very displeasing to God. This refusal to remember what the Lord had done for them over years and years was so ingrained in them that a whole generation was wiped out and never entered the promised land.

Complaining dwindles our faith because it makes our problems appear great and our God appear small. Complaining makes us believe in the lie that God will not help us. Complaining is a sign of unbelief and pride. Complaining makes us focus on our situation and fills us with self-pity. Gratitude does the opposite. As we remind ourselves of God's goodness and greatness, we have the assurance that He can and will do for us what He has done before.

Let's pause right now and take the time to express, in our own words, our gratitude to Him for life itself and for the many things we often take for granted.

Empathy, the result of going through

You could call it the missing ingredient. If you don't have this, you're not authentic to the people you reach out to. You come across as bland, like a good dish that lacks something you can't quite put your finger on. Empathy helps us to minister from a place of kindness and tenderness. Empathy is the capacity to understand what another person is experiencing from within that person's frame of reference. It is the capacity to put oneself in another person's shoes. Empathy doesn't come from reading a book or going on a course. It comes from going through a severe challenge and coming out on the other side of it. God promises us comfort with these words in 2 Corinthians 1:4 (NKJV): 'Who comforts us in all our tribulation that we may be able to comfort those who are in any trouble, with the comfort with which we ourselves are comforted by God.'

Empathy is that deep well you draw from to reach out to others in a hurting world. Facing the truth will expose the contents of your empathy well. Is it full, half-full, or empty? My well of empathy was very empty because I hadn't been through anything I could call a major challenge, neither as a child nor as an adult. Nothing as yet had happened to fill my well. God uses people who've been through challenges to help bring others through their own challenges. God uses people who go through and come out on the other side. When you ask God to use you to be a blessing in the lives of others, He has no choice but to check your empathy levels before releasing you out there. And if your levels are low or non-existent, He sets about ensuring that life events provide opportunities for a top-up or fill-up of this missing ingredient. God knows exactly what is required to bring about His purposes in us. And just in case we think all trouble comes from the devil and should be prayed away, remember our true ministry comes out of the things we've been through. Where does compassion come from? Where does perseverance come from? Where does pressing on come from? From the tests and trials we go through. His promise to us is that He will be with us *as* we go through. Isaiah 43:2 (NLT) says that, 'When you go through deep waters, I will be with you. When you go through rivers of difficulty, you will not drown. When you walk through the fire of oppression, you will not be burned up; the flames will not consume you.'

He will hold your hand as you walk through the fire. Notice the word says "when you walk through the fire" – how come we don't get to run through the fire but instead we walk through? It's because the fire is doing its work as we walk. He uses the fire to burn off the things that do not belong with us in the place where He is taking us.

God will always make sure that you have a personal connection to your call, that you know what it feels like and you know what it is like to walk a certain road. The people we reach out to or minister to can always sense empathy; they know that you know. It's not something you can fake, it's something you carry as a result of an experience. Empathy makes you authentic.

It is the very things we've been through that prepare us to be a blessing in someone else's life. Jesus had to go through challenging experiences so He could become our High Priest.

Hebrews 4:15 (NKJV) explains, 'For we do not have a High Priest who cannot sympathise with our weaknesses, but was in all points tempted as we are, yet without sin.' Jesus went through false accusation, being misunderstood, rejection, criticism, false accusation, being talked about, controversy, hatred, betrayal and humiliation. Why? So that He could be a

High Priest who was touched by the feeling of our infirmities. Hebrews 5:8 (NKJV) says, 'Though He was a Son, yet He learned obedience by the things which He suffered.' From age 12 to age 30 we never hear of Him except this statement in Luke 2:40 (NKJV) which says, 'And the Child grew and became strong in spirit, filled with wisdom; and the grace of God was upon Him.' Those were His "going through" years. We see that even Jesus had to go through a process before He could be released into His purpose.

Your destiny incorporates your pain. God will use you in the very area where you have experienced your greatest agony. All the while, we must bear in mind that Jeremiah 29:11 (NIV) encourages us:" For I know the plans I have for you," declares the Lord, "plans to prosper you and not to harm you, plans to give you hope and a future."'

Determine to push through because the things you have been through are what you will use to help others come through. As you go through, always choose who God says you are over who the enemy tries to convince you that you are because of your challenges. All through the twists and turns, He is weaving the tapestry of your life and you are being reformed to become who you were meant to be, fulfilling your destiny.

Say Goodbye to Your Own Way

The biggest hindrance to us becoming a vessel God can use is the self-life. It's wonderful to bask in His presence in worship and declare our undying love for Him. Like Peter, we can declare our undying loyalty to Christ until we are called upon to prove it and then find that we fail miserably. Peter did not know what was in his own heart until the crisis arose.

As we continue our journey of growing in Him, we will come face-to-face with this truth about self. Self is usually very much alive in us and revealing its presence in our choices, our priorities, our spending habits, our eating habits, our use of time and what we are willing to do or not do for Him. The challenge we face when it comes to fasting, praying for long hours, or experiencing any degree of discomfort in our pursuit of Him is an indication that self is still very much alive and kicking in us. This is the cross Jesus was referring to when He said in Mark 8:34 (NLT), 'If any of you wants to be my follower, you must give up your own way, take up your cross, and follow me.'

To be a follower you must give up your own way. The only way to deal with self is to kill it. Self must die – completely, totally. We must die to our way of making what we want, feel, or think guide our lives, so that we can become alive to being led by the Spirit of God. As believers, we are all called but only those willing to sacrifice self on the altar are chosen. There must be only one king reigning in our lives. Self cannot reign alongside the King of kings.

Jesus also spoke these words to demonstrate to us the productive power of this death to self, by likening it to the condition a seed must fulfil before it can bear any fruit. In John 12:24 (AMPC), He says, 'I assure you, most solemnly I tell you, unless a grain of wheat falls into the earth and dies, it remains [just one grain; it never becomes more but lives] by itself alone. But if it dies, it produces many others and yields a rich harvest.'

Our death to self is not an end in itself but rather it is the doorway into a fruitful life, not just for us but for many others. We die in order that Christ can manifest through us. We get self out of the way so that when we speak all they hear is Him and none of us. We die to self so that rivers of living water can flow out of us to others.

When a seed is planted, it is effectively dead and buried in the ground. It is all by itself with no access to any light for weeks. And yet, in the mystery of resurrection, that same seed emerges from the ground several weeks later, alive and full of fresh life, ready to grow and produce lots of fruit which, in turn, carries more seeds. Keep this picture in mind whenever circumstances seem to have buried you alive as it were. If your outward circumstances remain the same despite your many prayers, learn to recognise that God is doing a work in you that in time will lead to more fruit.

Self was being put to death when I experienced what it felt like to not have all the answers. I was unsure of myself, I didn't have enough money to pay my bills and I was stripped of all the things I had put my confidence in. God was doing internal works for eternal purposes. If I am really honest, I hated my life so much that, for a few days, I actually wanted to die but I quickly repented of that. There are times when we go through very devastating situations and we can feel so miserable that we hate our life and wish we were dead so that the misery can end. Make sure you don't allow yourself to entertain those thoughts and emotions. Make sure you don't voice out such emotions or dwell on such thoughts, not even once, because that is how we give the enemy ammunition to magnify them until they can become real suicidal thoughts or depression.

It is perfectly natural to want misery to cease, but we must never allow our thoughts to take us to a place of considering doing something about it because that is when we stray into the enemy's territory. Things may have looked the same on the outside but things were changing on the inside where it counts. He was killing off my pride and arrogance and building up humility in their place. He was killing off my selfishness and harshness and building up wells of compassion. He was killing off my self-dependence and building dependence on Him. The Potter was reforming the clay into a usable vessel. This caterpillar was morphing into a butterfly. The process was tough but necessary.

One way or another we get to learn this truth – that the official way to really know Him is through adversity and challenges. In the valley and not on the mountain top, in the lows and not the highs. Real change comes when He is able to get our full attention after we've run out of our own answers and solutions, after we've run out of steam, after we hit the brick wall, after we've tried everything else and failed. When there's no one else left but Him.

When the enemy comes in like a flood and all hell breaks loose. *When* and not *if* the storms of life hit.

When you walk through the fire. "When" means that it's just a matter of time, that it is inevitable and it is unavoidable. There's no point praying that the "whens" shouldn't happen or that they should be removed. Instead, we must focus on the promises He has given us when those seasons hit. Jesus prepared us for these seasons by saying in John 16:33(NKJV), 'These things I have spoken to you, that in Me you may have peace. In the world you will have tribulation; but be of good cheer, I have overcome the world.' It is through these "tribulations" that we really get to know Him. We learn to trust Him when we don't understand why. We learn to say, like Job, 'Though He slay me yet will I trust Him.' In 2 Corinthians 4:17 (NASB), Apostle Paul referred to the many difficult situations he encountered as "momentary light afflictions". Your wilderness season may take what seems like forever but you will emerge transformed.

We all need to reach a point when we are no longer afraid of dying to self – when we recognise that self is actually of no value but is rather a hindrance to us. You may think that you are losing a part of yourself, your personality, your individuality but actually, you are losing the things that you picked up along the way that were never meant to be part of you. By dying to self and giving up your own way, you are becoming who you really are – made in the image and likeness of God. You are being conformed not to the world but to the image of Christ.

I challenge you to give up your own way and die to self so that, like the grain of wheat that is planted in the earth and dies, you can go from abiding alone to bearing lots of fruit.

If you're ready, take a deep breath and let's pray this together: *Lord, I finally recognise that the only way to have more of You is to have less of me. I choose to surrender to You and to say no to self. I ask You for the grace to continue to yield to You in every area of my life knowing and trusting You to hold my hand all the way. In Jesus' name, Amen.*

PART TWO
Growing pains

GETTING RID OF OUR EXCESS BAGGAGE

(we all have a lot!)

As the caterpillar grows, it sheds its outer covering. Without this shedding, it cannot grow. It is this shedding that liberates it from the previous life stage and prepares it for the next stage of growth.

You can't win any race with excess weights tied to your legs. We each have an endurance race to run and if we want to obtain the prize then we must get rid of every dead weight in order to run our race successfully. Hebrews 12:1 (NKJV) says, 'Therefore we also, since we are surrounded by so great a cloud of witnesses, let us lay aside every weight, and the sin which so easily ensnares us, and let us run with endurance the race that is set before us.' We will need to recognise any weights we are carrying such as unforgiveness, offence, and dishonour, and lay them aside so that we can become useable.

Fulfilling our destinies is always tied to three things – people, place and time. Destiny-destroyers are simply the devices the enemy uses to divert us from these three things and stop us from fulfilling our destinies. In 2 Corinthians 2:11 (NKJV), it says '… Lest Satan should take advantage of us; for we are not ignorant of his devices.' We must not walk around ignorant of his devices and his attempts to derail us.

Pride, offence, unforgiveness and lack of honour are destiny-destroyers that can successfully move us away from people, place and time in one fell swoop.

PRIDE STINKS TO GOD

A Journey out of the land called pride

I used to think I was the best when the truth is I wasn't, not at all. I was full of pride and arrogance and I had no idea. Pride is very deceptive and I really thought I was humble when I was actually very proud. Pride stops us from fulfilling our destiny. Pride is the chief destiny-destroyer. Pride takes many forms but it is always rooted in self – in me, myself, and I. Pride is a type of excess baggage that must never travel with us anywhere ever! Pride will make you depend on yourself - your ability, your looks, your connections, your money, or your strength. Pride says, "I don't need God, I can do it myself". The book of Proverbs contains many scriptures on the folly of pride. Proverbs 16:18 (NKJV) declares that, 'Pride goes before destruction, and a haughty spirit before a fall.' We must not feed pride but starve it instead. We must never ever forget that pride and arrogance stink to God. Pride was the reason Lucifer was thrown out of heaven!

Proverbs 6:17-19 (NKJV) lists seven things the Lord hates and the first one listed is "a proud look". Apostle Peter spells it out further in 1 Peter 5:5 (NKJV) by saying, 'God resists the proud, but gives grace to the humble.' Stop for a moment and consider that God resists us when we are proud. When God Himself is resisting us, nothing can possibly go well until we deal with our pride.

Pride stops you accepting help you need

Pride stopped me from accepting help when it was being offered. The first time someone gave me a financial gift when my crisis first began, I politely refused it. All I could think was, *Is this what I have been reduced to?* I was too proud to receive something I badly needed. Imagine how silly that is. But that's pride for you.

Ecclesiastes 3:1 says there is a season and time for everything. This means there is a time to take a break from trying to do everything, especially when we are emotionally fragile. I didn't want to accept help of any kind – not even prayer. To me, needing prayer meant that I wasn't coping well, that I didn't have it together and that I was crumbling under the pressure. It meant that people would know I had problems and start feeling sorry for me. I continued to project my "tough woman" mindset, even though inside I was disintegrating and a complete mess.

I thought opening up to share my innermost feelings with anyone was a sign of weakness. My default was to help others but never to be seen as needing any kind of help. I called it "being strong" and "holding things together". I called it "not crumbling under pressure". Pride was my biggest problem and I was completely unaware of it.

Eventually, with God's help, I woke up to the truth that had been staring at me all along. Help was available and I needed to learn to receive it when it was offered and to ask for it when I needed it, too. I finally put aside the false persona and humbled myself to accept the help I badly needed. Instead of viewing help as an indication of how bad things had become in my life, I began to see it for what it was – a sign of God's love and care for me. Pride never pays for your groceries at the supermarket or pays your mortgage, but unsolicited financial gifts from family and friends do. I dropped the pride and began to accept the gifts I was being offered because they truly were answers to prayer. In that season, I learnt to stop thinking I could depend on myself. I learnt how to totally depend on Him for my financial needs and God came through each time without fail. I never had to go and ask anyone for money and I never had to borrow. He always sent help just when I needed it.

Seasons of great financial challenge, of not having any solutions for our predicament, open us up to growing in faith that God will always provide. They are opportunities to know Him as our source, as Jehovah Jireh – the Lord who provides. What was the outcome of that season of being on my own, of being so broke with two teenage daughters and a mortgage and bills to pay? Pride and self-sufficiency gave way to humility and dependence on God. He opened the way for me to understand what true humility was. To understand that being real isn't weakness and humility is strength, not weakness.

We all need our support networks. Psalm 68:6 (NIV) puts it very simply: 'God sets the lonely in families.' We need our church sisters and brothers – our church family. We need our biological family to support us through life's storms. We need our close friends to rally around us in a crisis. We must never let our pride stop us from accepting their support and help in whatever form it takes. There are times when our strength is depleted and God sends others to support our hands until we are recharged.

In Exodus 17:8-13 we read that the Israelites were fighting the Amalekites and as long as Moses held up his hands, the Israelites were winning, but whenever he lowered his hands, the Amalekites were winning. When Moses' hands grew tired, Aaron and Hur supported his hands, one on each side. His hands were steady until the going down of the sun and they overcame the Amalekites. We all need our Aaron and Hur to hold up our hands when we can't hold them up ourselves anymore. Don't push your helpers away. Don't refuse help because you feel you're being a burden and don't cut them off in a bid to protect your so-called tough image. They are sent by God to lighten the load.

Not sharing our challenges with anyone is also a form of pride! It means we are relying only on ourselves for solutions. We must learn to be humble enough to ask for help when we need it and then be humble enough to receive the help when it comes because it is all part of God taking care of us.

Pride comes in many shapes and sizes

When the Lord began to show me that my biggest issue was that of pride, it came as a shock. He showed me various scenarios of my dealings with others, which were often insensitive, from a place of feeling superior in intelligence, and very often unkind.

I was in the middle of a week-long fast and had been asking the Lord what it was about me that needed to change. I prayed this prayer from Psalm 139:23-24 (AMPC): 'Search me [thoroughly], O God, and know my heart! Try me and know my thoughts! And see if there is any wicked or hurtful way in me, and lead me in the way everlasting.'

I kept hearing one word – *pride*. I thought I didn't hear it right. Me, proud? Never! I considered myself nice and friendly because I got along well with most people. The Lord began to break down my pride issues to me in great detail. It went like this: *You've always found it easy to make friends and so you often say you don't understand anyone who is a loner and socially awkward. You've always been good with figures so you say you don't understand anyone who can't do excel spreadsheets. Who gave you your brain?* God continued to point out my areas of pride, such as my inability to understand why people didn't accept the gospel the first time they heard it and my judgement of women who had made poor choices in relationships. At the end of all of this, I heard Him say, *I would never do that. I always reach out to people where they are and then I help them up. How can I use you if this is what you would say to the people I send you to?*

By this time, I was so convicted that tears were just flowing down my face, as He had perfectly described my behaviour – I had never considered this as pride! For the first time, I came face-to-face with the truth about pride in me and it was not a pretty picture. Be careful what you pray for and be ready to hear the truth. I hadn't realised that I was prideful about my abilities and scornful about the lack of ability in others. I repented and asked the Lord to help me change and be more like Him. I asked Him to help me accept people as they are and not judge them regardless of any poor choices they may have made.

This began a period of God working pride, in its many forms, out of me. Nice, friendly, chat-with-anyone me was actually full of pride. For a number of years after that encounter, whenever I asked the Lord what needed to change about me, I would still hear the same word – pride. I would remark, *But, Lord, we did pride last year so surely, we can move on to something else.* All He would do was show me another aspect of my character which I had never viewed as pride and we would work on it that year. Over time, slowly but surely, I became very conscious of my wrong habits and, with the help of the Holy Spirit, I learnt to slow down, appreciate the difference in others and value that difference.

We may be absolutely useless at listening to others, impatient with anyone who doesn't move or think at the same fast pace that we do. We may have a habit of finishing off sentences for whomever we are speaking with because they speak slowly or are not so articulate. Or we may be at the other end of the pride spectrum where we hide from the spotlight and run from any attempt to make us shine and we call it being humble. Whichever end of the pride spectrum we find ourselves, the focus of pride is always me, me and me. Unless we allow pride to be killed off, we will be carrying excess baggage that will hinder our destiny fulfilment.

God has wired us all differently because we each have a unique purpose and He will not wire us with what we do not require to fulfil that purpose. Some of us are wired to take life at a slower pace, enjoy the journey and stop to help lots of people as we go. We may be called to be a voice of encouragement to others, blessed with a soft heart so that we find it easy to feel for others. We must not view someone else who is wired to be a trailblazing entrepreneur as taking life too fast and consider them mean for not stopping to help every single person they meet, or vice versa. We must value the uniqueness of everyone and not wish they were more like us, or we like them.

Pride hides

We can easily think we are fine when we are anything but! Our own hearts deceive us by not telling us the truth but the Holy Spirit will always reveal the truth to us. He may tell us directly or use someone close to tell us. Pride hides and once we recognise how deadly it is, we must determine not to allow any pride to remain in us. We must be ruthless in dealing with it by first asking the Lord to reveal any hidden pride in us. We must find the courage to identify someone who regularly speaks good counsel into our lives to be on the lookout for any signs of pride in our attitude. It could be a mentor, your spouse, or a close friend – someone who knows you well and loves you enough to speak the truth to you in love. The question then is – how good are you at receiving what they tell you? Pride can make us try to deflect or deny the truth we are being told.

The day I realised that I had no such person doing that in my life, it scared me no end. Being the rather strong personality that I was, even when a close friend would point things out that I could do differently, I was quick to explain why they were wrong. I would say that I did not agree with them and reject whatever feedback I had received. This was a very dangerous place to be.

After toying with this for a few months (yes, months), I finally made the decision to ask my small group leader, who was also my pastor, if she would take on the task. I felt a bit awkward but I went ahead anyway and told her I felt I needed to give her permission to speak into my life whenever she saw anything in me that needed correcting or adjusting. Her response was totally not what I expected. First, she said, 'This is the best thing I have heard you say to me in the 14 years that I have known you! Do you know how many times I needed to tell you something and I taught it to the whole group because I knew that was the only way you would receive it?' This is when I began to learn to receive feedback gracefully and humbly and to even ask for it so that I could become a better person. Pride will quickly run out of hiding places as we learn to identify it and root it out.

Pride never gives up and will attempt to hide behind good gestures, good character traits, and good actions. That is why we must continue to ask God to search our hearts and examine our motives. It's so easy to do something good but with the wrong motive. We must never think we have arrived when it comes to the issue of pride because it will always attempt to rear its ugly head in another area. Pride is something we need to be constantly on the lookout for in our lives, especially if we have a lot of natural ability. It is so easy to think it has something to do with us but what do we have that was not given to us? Let us continually ask the Holy Spirit to shine His light in our hearts and show us if there is any pride lurking anywhere so that we can root it out.

Pride makes you judgemental

When it comes to judging others, what you give is what you get. Jesus spoke in no uncertain terms about the blindness and hypocrisy associated with being judgemental and the dangers of judging others by our own poor standards unless we want to be judged accordingly. Jesus warned us in Matthew 7:1-2 (AMPC), 'Do not judge and criticise and condemn others, so that you may not be judged and criticised and condemned yourselves. For just as you judge and criticise and condemn others, you will be judged and criticised and condemned, and in accordance with the measure you [use to] deal out to others, it will be dealt out again to you.' The Bible is telling us that we should not judge, otherwise we, too, will be judged and we will be judged with the same measure we use to judge others. That's pretty scary – for God to judge me based on the way

I judge others. I cannot judge rightly when my judgment lacks mercy, lacks compassion, and, above all, lacks full knowledge. Only God knows someone's full story and that is why only He can sit as judge.

I had never struggled with making poor decisions or been weak when it comes to diligence and so I would end up judging others based on my own narrow viewpoint and opinions. Why can't they be strong? Why are they so forgetful or so disorganised? Why do they always pick a loser to go out with? I couldn't relate to the normal faults of the people around me. Because I did not suffer from those particular shortcomings, I actually thought it meant I had none. I never thought that I was judging them and opening myself to being judged by the same measure.

In my journey out of pride, God showed me the danger of being judgemental. I am forever grateful to Him for opening my eyes to this terrible default I had. Now I am much more alert to this and stop myself from passing judgement on the actions of others. I have learnt to zip up and not voice my opinion on anyone's faults. I am not their judge, God is. Plus, I now recognise I have several faults of my own and I need to focus on dealing with my own planks not the specks of others!

If this happens to be one of your defaults, when you encounter anyone with all kinds of "shortcomings", do not sit as a judge because you do not know what has happened in their lives that has resulted in the behaviour. Only God has everyone's full story and that is why only He can judge righteously. James 4:12 (NLT) cautions us, 'God alone, who gave the law, is the Judge. He alone has the power to save or to destroy. So what right do you have to judge your neighbour?'

God delivered me from pride and its associated issues of being insensitive, unkind, harsh, judgemental, self-righteous, and thinking I know everything. It has been a journey-and-a-half and I am still on that journey. The difference is that I am much more self-aware and on the alert for any signs of it so that I can stamp it out fast.

Has any of this resonated with you? Have you felt that the Holy Spirit was highlighting a default or a behaviour that you need to address?

Don't ignore it, let's pray and deal with it now: *Father, I come before You in the name of Jesus and I repent of pride in me. I repent of pride in the way I think and behave towards others. Forgive me and cleanse me of pridefulness. Lord, by Your Spirit, I ask You to make me instantly alert whenever I exhibit pride in any form so that I can address it immediately. Create in me a clean heart, oh Lord, so that I can receive more grace from You to live humbly before You and others. In Jesus' name, Amen.*

THE PRISON OF UNFORGIVENESS

Let it go – let them go – forgive

Stop the thief in his tracks before he grabs anything else. Whatever may have happened to you, refuse to become a casualty of the enemy. John 10:10 (NKJV) gives us Satan's mission: 'The thief does not come except to steal, and to kill, and to destroy.'

Forgiveness is probably one of the toughest lessons we have to learn as we mature in our Christian walk. The enemy may have stolen your innocence, your relationships or even robbed you of your family. If you do not forgive, then you give him the opportunity to go further to kill and destroy your destiny. The only way to stop the enemy in his tracks is through forgiveness. Forgive those who hurt, judged, betrayed, abused or abandoned you. No matter the situation, for your own sake, let them go. Forgive them – all of them.

Unforgiveness is huge because it's one of the biggest and heaviest forms of our excess baggage. The weight of unforgiveness will prevent you from moving forward into your destiny.

Unforgiveness can make you ill

When my marriage fell apart, I was angry. I felt betrayed. I felt wronged. I was vengeful and felt I had every right to feel the way I did and maintain the position I'd taken. As a "good" Christian, I knew I had to let it go but I was still looking for revenge and for justice and I secretly hoped God would do it for me. I felt someone had to pay for what had happened to me. I was miserable yet very focused on my justification of my self-righteous position. Are we ever justified? Never! Because we all sin. We may have been hurt but remember we also hurt others.

Throughout that period, my health had been deteriorating as I was experiencing heart problems, particularly serious palpitations. I couldn't even watch the news without feeling like my heart was doing huge summersaults inside me. At its height, the doctor suggested that I have a pacemaker fitted so that I could function more normally. I was holding so much resentment and unforgiveness that it was making me ill and I had no idea this was the cause.

How many of us say all kinds of strong prayers binding the devil's attacks or praying for healing when the real remedy is simply to forgive and let the person go? Learning to practice true forgiveness became my ticket away from having a pacemaker fitted to my heart. The Lord in His mercy led me to an understanding of forgiveness and of the power of blessing, and why He commands us to forgive.

Forgiveness stops the rot

Unforgiveness is toxic on several levels. As the saying goes – it's like drinking poison and thinking it's the other person who is going to die. Unforgiveness was the cause of my heart problems and it is the cause of many diseases in the body. Forgiveness is God's antibiotic for clearing the infection caused by the hurt. When you hold on to resentment, it feels like there's a war going on inside you because you're in a battle with yourself, as well as others. Unforgiveness is extremely high maintenance. The more you fight, the more ground you lose. Arguing just drains you of energy and leaves you angrier and more hurt. You're in a no-win situation. You struggle with who's right and who's wrong. You spend so much time trying to outdo, out-shout, and out-manoeuvre others that you lose your peace and joy. You lose your sleep thinking about what you said, should have said, could have said, while the person who hurt you is fast asleep. Let *them* (those who hurt you) go by letting *it* (what they did) go. End the conflict now! Refuse to live this way another day. Don't allow someone's actions to determine your reactions. We are to forgive because we have been forgiven a debt we could never ever repay.

The Power of Blessing

You know forgiveness is complete when you can bless those who hurt you from your heart.

Jesus was teaching us an entirely different way to deal with life's hurts when He said in Luke 6: 27-28 (NKJV), 'But I say to you who hear: Love your enemies, do good to those who hate you, bless those who curse you, and pray for those who spitefully use you.'

It was no longer an eye for an eye and a tooth for tooth, rather we are to extend mercy and not require justice. Instead of seeking revenge when someone hurts us, He tells us to respond to them with love. He asks us to be good to them, to bless and pray for them. He doesn't say we should wait until they apologise or admit they were wrong. He doesn't say we should wait until we feel good and it doesn't hurt anymore. This is totally contrary to our natural response when someone does something to hurt us. We want justice, we want an apology, we want them to acknowledge their wrong. We want payback in some way. As Christians, we do our best to obey by declaring that we have forgiven but very often the wounds remain in the form of painful memories and protective walls we erect to prevent further hurt.

Jesus was teaching us that the way to healing and complete wholeness is by praying for and blessing the person who hurt us instead. To bless is to speak God's favour or intention on someone. To bless is to speak well of someone. Blessing is the opposite of cursing. Praying and blessing is the way to recover fully from a painful experience. It is the way to stop the experience from causing further damage to us. Blessing is the way of ensuring we do not carry it as excess baggage into the rest of our relationships in life.

I learnt to apply this first-hand when, out of the blue, and in a time of great tensions, my husband turned up at church one Sunday. He had only attended a few times in the previous ten years. At that time, I was in a terrible state and saw it as a deliberate invasion of my only safe space. It was very awkward; my church was suddenly now his church and I found it so difficult that I felt I had no choice but to leave my beloved church. One night I cried out to the Lord for His help because I simply didn't know what to do anymore. The next morning, my sisters called to say she had heard someone on TBN teaching about the power of blessing and about how I needed to forgive my husband, pray for him, bless him, and also go back to church! I remember thinking to myself, *Bless him? You must be joking!* Everything within me wanted to fight the idea yet I knew straight away that God was answering my prayer from the night before. It was up to me to obey the instruction or not obey and remain in my desperate predicament.

I decided to obey and pray the opposite of all the awful things I had been wishing on him. I prayed for him all that day and made a decision to pray for him daily. I tied the new habit to my morning shower so that I would always remember to pray for him. I also decided to go back to church that Sunday, whether he was there or not, and called the church office to inform them. The administrator said I had been on the rota to give the offering talk that Sunday but had arranged for someone else to do it in my absence. I told him to put me back on as I would be there to do it. I went to church that Sunday dressed in my favourite colour, red, (as you do) and gave the talk and, yes, he was there but I was on a roll. I was walking out my new revelation about praying for those who have treated you badly and blessing them and nothing was going to stop me.

Forgiveness has many rewards

Jesus carries on with His teaching in Luke 6: 35-36 (NKJV) by saying, 'But love your enemies, do good, and lend, hoping for nothing in return; and your reward will be great, and you will be sons of the Most High. For He is kind to the unthankful and evil. Therefore, be merciful, just as your Father also is merciful.' As I continued to practice my new praying and blessing habit there was an immediate change in my circumstances. First of all, exactly seven days after I began, I received a gift of £7,000 in my account! Next, exactly eight days later, my ex-husband calls our younger daughter and announces that he has decided that he will no longer be attending our church and will look for another church. Then, on top of it all, about three months later, as I continued this new practice of praying for those who spitefully use you, I noticed that all the heart palpitations had completely ceased! My heart was no longer doing summersaults inside me. I could watch the news or a movie in peace and I no longer needed a pacemaker.

I finally understood what I had been doing to myself by holding all that resentment and unforgiveness inside me against someone. I continued this daily practice for a whole year and gained great peace in the process,

I learnt to be like my Father, who is kind to everyone and I received several rewards, too. When I practiced total forgiveness my finances improved, my health improved, and my peace returned.

But it's not fair

Making the decision to let it go and let them go is probably one of the toughest decisions you will ever make. Forgiveness is often a huge struggle for many of us because, somehow, forgiveness looks like letting the perpetrator get off scot-free and it just seems so unfair. Some of us have been through horrific situations and experiences and forgiveness makes it seem like what happened to us doesn't matter. Of course it matters that we have suffered terribly. It matters that we have endured unimaginable pain. We feel justified in holding on to unforgiveness, but in doing so we not only hold on to the pain, we also carry all the negative effects of that experience into our future. We must acknowledge that pain and bring it before God and let Him heal us of every trauma we have suffered and every wound we have sustained.

Practicing forgiveness is about ensuring that the enemy does not get to wreak further destruction in our lives.

We cannot undo what has happened but we can make sure it does not continue its destructive goal. Forgiveness is about ensuring that we do not carry that extra baggage around with us. We forgive because we have been forgiven a much larger debt. It wasn't fair that Jesus paid the price for our sins but He willingly laid down His life so that we can be free. The Lord's Prayer has a line where it says "forgive us our trespasses even as we forgive those who trespass against us". We will be forgiven according to the measure we forgive others. Unforgiveness means that God also will not forgive us our own sins and who among us doesn't need forgiveness?

Vengeance belongs to God not us

You may be asking, 'But what about the wrong done to me?' Rest assured, it has not been forgotten. Galatians 6:7(NKJV) says, 'Do not be deceived, God is not mocked; for whatever a man sows, that he will also reap.' Payback always comes, just not from you. There's only one qualified judge; we are told to let Him handle it. Romans 12:19 (NKJV) puts it this way: 'Beloved, do not avenge yourselves, but rather give place to wrath; for it is written, "Vengeance is Mine, I will repay," says the Lord.' We must do our part and let Him do His part. Our part is to hand the person over to the judge and concentrate on releasing forgiveness and getting healed.

Let's start with this simple prayer: *Lord, I'm angry. Please help me to let it go. I ask You to help me to release my anger, turn the other cheek, and forgive the one who has done me wrong. In Jesus' name, Amen.*

Choose freedom

Forgiveness is a decision not a feeling. We forgive others because we also have been forgiven much. Unforgiveness means we have forgotten that we have been forgiven. We forgive others because we also need to be forgiven. Nobody is perfect so we all need God's forgiveness on an ongoing basis. Unforgiveness shuts up the heavens above us and our prayers are not heard but forgiveness puts us back in the will of God.

Unforgiveness means that we are handed over to the torturer until we pay. Can we pay for what Christ has done for us? Can we ever repay an unpayable debt? Choosing to forgive sets us free from the torturer. Choosing forgiveness means we refuse to let Satan win.

Releasing forgiveness lets the love and peace of God fill our minds so much that it overflows to others – including those who have hurt us. Stop and think: do you really want to become like the person who hurt you? Jesus did not retaliate or look for payback against those who inflicted so much pain on Him. He chose to pray for the people nailing Him to the cross. He prayed for His enemies as He instructed us to.

If you make the decision to choose freedom, then let's pray this prayer: *Lord, I choose to be merciful. I choose to obey You and practice forgiveness. I release [xxxx] from every wrong they have done to me. I place them in Your hands and I release them from any debt they owe me and I choose to bless them. Thank You, Lord, for giving me the grace to forgive the person who hurt me and to follow You. In Jesus' name, Amen.*

OFFENCE – THE BLESSING BLOCKER

Whatever you do, don't take the bait

Satan doesn't come wearing a red jumpsuit and horns as depicted in story books because if he did, we would all see him coming. He specialises in stealth and deception. Offence is the devil's bait. It places us in the playground of the enemy. It is a major destiny-destroyer and is one of the devil's choice weapons of destruction. Offence is excess baggage that will throw us off course in our journey. It leads to division in churches, families, nations and relationships. Offence opens the door to every kind of evil work. Offence is Satan's bait, which he uses to lure us into his trap and then he pounces. So, whatever you do, "don't take the bait!" And here's why.

Offence blinds us

When we are offended, all we see is what has been done to us. We are the victim, and we become all self-righteous and blind to the fact that in the Kingdom of God, the wrongdoer will be judged for their wrong *and* the wronged will also be judged for their wrong response to the original wrong! The God we serve causes the rain to fall on both the evil and the good. The God we serve does not deal with us as we deserve. He warns us not to seek to vindicate ourselves in such situations but to respond right and leave the vindicating to Him. He is the righteous judge; He knows the full story and we don't. All we know is that we have been on the receiving end of someone's actions. In 1 Peter 5:8 (NKJV), we're told, 'Be sober, be vigilant; because your adversary the devil walks about like a roaring lion, seeking whom he may devour.'

Satan is walking around looking for someone to destroy – why present yourself? Offence gives the lion open access to come and devour you. It is an open invitation that says to the lion, "come and get me, you can have me for dinner". Offence gives the enemy license to come and ruin your home and relationships. It gives the enemy license to come and steal your health, peace, and strength.

The devil likes to throw the arrow of offence when other arrows he has thrown to get you off course have failed. Personally, I believe it is the choicest arrow in his bag of fiery darts. He always bides his time and waits for an opportune moment, a time when you are weak, vulnerable, suffering a trauma, loss, or bereavement – that is when he pounces. This is what the apostle Peter, was warning us about in the above scripture. Offence makes us easy prey for the roaring lion. We become one of the ones he may devour.

Offence entices you into Satan's trap!

Offence causes you to walk right into Satan's trap. It is a major means of self-sabotage and destiny destruction. Just as with any trap, the bait is enticing, it gives no indication of danger and we are unaware of how dangerous offence is until we're caught in it. Apostle Paul says in Ephesians 4:27 (AMPC), 'Leave no [such] room or foothold for the devil [give no opportunity to him].' Offence gives a legal foothold and victory to the devil.

I was already hurting, smarting from the wounds and knocks of separation and divorce. I was already in the middle of a storm. I was juggling roles, parenting teenagers with more month than money, and trying to be a good leader in my church – that is when the enemy threw this arrow at me. Initially, it was just the interfering do-gooders quoting their scriptures at me, telling me that God hates divorce and that I was outside the will of God. Some even had "prophetic words", given by God to them for me, that my business was failing because I had broken up with my husband. There were numerous "offence opportunities" and I was taking the bait. The list of people on my offence list was growing. The enemy was having a field day and I was totally oblivious to the fact that I was walking into a trap laid for me. And then, as if things couldn't get any worse, he proceeded to lure me further into the offence trap.

Offence distorts the truth

Offence will distort the truth and steal your testimony. Offence will cause you to sever your destiny connections and turn your back on key relationships. It causes you to have amnesia. You forgot all the good things associated with the relationship and only focus on what went wrong. John the Baptist was Jesus' cousin, he had baptised Him and seen the Holy Spirit descend on Him like a dove. He understood Jesus was the Messiah to the extent that he said in John 3:30 (NKJV), 'He must increase but I must decrease.' Later, however, John the Baptist ended up being imprisoned by Herod. Who knows, maybe he was upset that Jesus had not come to visit him or perhaps he felt Jesus could have done something to get him out of prison. Matthew 11: 2 –6 (NKJV) tells us that, 'When John had heard in prison about the works of Christ, he sent two of his disciples and said to Him, "Are You the Coming One, or do we look for another?" Jesus answered and said to them, "Go and tell John the things which you hear and see:

The blind see and the lame walk; the lepers are cleansed and the deaf hear; the dead are raised up and the poor have the gospel preached to them. And blessed is he who is not offended because of Me."

Whatever it was, doubt and offence had crept into John's heart and came out of his mouth and turned into action. Offence turned John the Baptist from the one who baptised Jesus and witnessed the Holy Spirit descend on Him in confirmation, to the one sending two of his men to ask Jesus if He was indeed the Messiah!

Offence will cause you to dishonour your leaders without thinking that what you are doing is displeasing to God and therefore a sin. Offence makes you think you're right in your sin and stops you from repenting for your wrong response. Offence brings division and can destroy longstanding relationships by the seeds of discord we sow as we go around telling our "sympathisers" how we have been wronged. Jesus made this statement in John 14:30 (NKJV): 'I will no longer talk much with you, for the ruler of this world is coming, and he has nothing in Me.' Satan couldn't touch Jesus because He wasn't carrying any of his "stuff" but Satan was able to strike John the Baptist because he found some of his stuff (offence) in him.

I cannot stress it enough. Offence is a deadly virus and it is highly infectious! Don't get infected by it, and if you do, be quick to deal with it. Whatever you do, make sure you don't turn into a virus-spreader either! Don't help Satan fulfil his mission of accusing the brethren. Revelation 12:10 NKJV) reveals, 'For the accuser of our brethren, who accused them before our God day and night, has been cast down.' Remember Satan is a legalist. He is the accuser of the brethren and he never stops. Offence gives the enemy the legal right to accuse you before God. We must not give him ammunition that he can legally use against us to block answers to our prayers or put sickness and disease on us. Remember Satan came to steal, to kill, and to destroy.

Offence is a displacer

How many of us have left our church and gone to another because we were hurt, and often by a leader? How many of us ever admitted to ourselves that we were offended? Me, offended? Never. *I was just hurt*, we say to ourselves and get on with our lives when all the while we are carrying the offence in our hearts.

I found myself caught up in some issues that involved a pastor from another ministry making some allegations to one of our leaders, who had no reason to disbelieve them. Over a period, the leader, in turn, made several remarks to me which I found very hurtful and things became really difficult. I was so hurt and confused about it all and felt betrayed by this leader who, of course, had no idea how I felt. This went on for several months. Somehow, I never mentioned the matter to my prayer partner or told other people how insensitive I felt this leader had been, or tried to share my side of the story. I believe God restrained me from going around telling my sob story even though I was very hurt and offended. No one is discounting the fact that, knowingly or unknowingly, the actions of our leaders can sometimes cause much hurt. We can find ourselves in situations where we are so bent on proving our point that love and honour fly out of the window. It's a slippery slope and Hebrews 12:15 (NLT) warns us to, 'Watch out that no poisonous root of bitterness grows up to trouble you, corrupting many.' Offence has a wide reach in terms of the damage it can cause around us, way beyond the individuals involved. Whatever the offence opportunity, we must be keenly aware that we should not react the way our emotions are telling us to.

Be led by the Holy Spirit, not your feelings

As the situation continued, I would simply pray, Lord, I don't want any trouble with you or your staff *so please just deal with me*. It was not a very deep prayer but it meant I was taking the matter to God and not saying anything that could corrupt many others. Instead of taking the enemy's bait, we must respond as the Word tells us to. We must report the servant to their boss (God) and let Him deal with them. We must be led by the Spirit and not by our feelings. Somehow, I could tell that this battle was spiritual and it was pointless to address it with an emotional response.

It was during that season God gave me the analogy that in any church, some people are pillars and some are bricks. Offence comes to displace you from the place where you belong. Pillars are custom-made specifically for a particular structure. Pillars are bespoke and designed to hold a structure up. Bricks, on the other hand, are generally always the same size, mass-produced with little variation in colour or density. A brick could leave church and slot easily into another church. A brick's departure wouldn't leave a huge dent or affect the structure. A pillar, however, has to think twice about leaving the place where they are planted. Pillars can't leave just because things have become very unpleasant. Pillars hold part of the structure up, if a pillar is removed without the provision of an adequate alternative, you damage the structure. Since a pillar is made specifically for a particular structure, a pillar will find it very hard to fit anywhere else.

Are you a pillar or a brick? That is something you need to work out for yourself. If you were the devil, would you try to displace a pillar or a brick from a church? I knew I was a pillar within my church and so despite the difficult situation, I needed to remain in place. I began to see the situation for what it was, an arrow sent to displace me from my purpose. It's important to know which one you are, a pillar or a brick. Don't let the enemy trap you with his bait of offence and then displace you from your destiny. Let us not be ignorant of the enemy's tactics. Don't let offence tempt you to cut and run from your church. This lesson is for pillars who want to fulfil their purpose. Offence comes to cut you off from the destiny connectors God has put in your life to help you to fulfil your purpose. Offence comes to displace you from the very place God has ordained for you to flourish and fulfil destiny. Lastly, offence comes to displace you from the timing of God.

By taking you out of the place where you should be and from the people you should be with, you miss your season for what God has planned for you. You must refuse every opportunity to be offended because it is a choice arrow of the enemy. Whatever you do, don't take the bait because offences come to throw you off course from your purpose permanently, or at the very least delay its fulfilment. Refuse to eat the devil's cheese. He uses it to lure us into his trap and then he pounces, rubbing his hands together gleefully as he sings "another one bites the dust".

If you recognise any kind of offence at anyone, great or small – stop now and make things right before Him.

Don't rehearse it, release it

I kept praying that simple prayer as I fought the battle between my ears. Why would a church leader behave like this? Shouldn't they know better? I became consumed with it all. For months, whenever I woke up, this was the first thing that came to mind. I noticed that I struggled to receive whenever this leader preached. I kept going over and over it in my mind – I was offended and I was feeding it by becoming obsessed with the matter. Before long, I was at the point where

I didn't want to have anything to do with church leaders generally. I started to believe that you had to be wary of them all unless you wanted to get hurt. Yet all along, I didn't think for a moment that I was offended.

Offence causes us to make incorrect generalisations and tar everyone with the same brush. One bad run-in with a mother-in-law and offence says every mother-in-law is evil. This was unfamiliar territory because, being naturally forthright, I wasn't one to avoid confronting issues head-on. I didn't harbour grudges only because I would quickly confront the person. Except, this time, my usual method wasn't going to work without being dishonouring. I couldn't confront them, say my piece, let off steam and get it over and done with. All the while, I continued praying my simple prayer. First, I had to accept that I was offended. Next, I had to accept that I couldn't fix this one myself and that I had to let go and trust God to do the fixing for me. This was extremely painful to my flesh, my sense of justice, and my feeling of being unfairly treated.

God will fix it if you hand it over

If we hand over the matter to God, He will always fix it and love will win if we recognise the trap set out for us and stick it out without trying to get people to hear our side and sympathise with us. We shouldn't go around point-scoring and sowing seeds in the minds of others in our bid for justice. We shouldn't try to vindicate ourselves but rather leave things in God's hands so that love always wins. Love is the restrainer and love never fails. The truth did finally come out and everything was sorted out. Love won and all the relationships were restored. I even received an apology. Once I learnt to let go of my offence and forgive, I was able to receive again from that leader and the other pastor's ministry once again. It didn't happen overnight. And I didn't find it easy to do. Everything in my flesh was screaming loudly, 'It's not right!' I had to extend total forgiveness to them. I had to acknowledge that, while I felt I had been wronged, my response to the wrong was just as wrong.

Let us pray: *Lord, I thank You for opening my eyes to the dangers of offence. Please forgive me for taking offence, and for taking Satan's bait. I release every form of resentment from my heart. I choose to respond to offences with Your love – I will not react with emotions but respond with love. Lord, give me the grace to refuse every offence opportunity so that I can fulfil all of my destiny. In Jesus' name, Amen.*

LACK OF HONOUR

A culture of honour

God loves people, all people, and He takes it personally when we don't show honour to people. We live in a world where it is considered acceptable, and even fashionable, to challenge authority figures. The current culture we live in says it's okay to dishonour. It's okay to dishonour every authority figure – police, parents, teachers, politicians, prime ministers, pastors, even God Himself! We give our leaders nicknames, sometimes derogatory, and talk about them in derision. We dissect their actions and lives and we consider it our duty to criticise them whenever we disagree with them. It is as though there is something within us that grates at the idea of honouring people. Dishonouring others by criticising and trivialising them is nothing but our own pride speaking. When we dishonour others, we are simply exposing the state of our own hearts. Dishonour shows up in sarcasm, criticism, lack of recognition, disrespect, in our heart attitudes, and in our actions. It is another major destiny-destroyer that we cannot afford to carry with us on our journey of transformation.

The Kingdom of God has a culture graced with honour and respect for the dignity of all people. The Bible calls God's kingdom the Kingdom of Light and calls Satan's kingdom the Kingdom of Darkness. If honour is the domain of the Kingdom of Light, then dishonour is the domain of the Kingdom of Darkness.

When we do not observe Kingdom principles, we will always pay the price, just as a violation of the law in any country has its repercussions. Many times, we are busy blaming the devil for situations not changing in our lives when it is often because we have violated Kingdom principles and have not repented of them. The Bible talks about the little foxes that spoil the vine in Songs of Solomon 2:15 (NKJV): 'Catch us the foxes, the little foxes that spoil the vines, for our vines have tender grapes.' Jesus said He is the vine and we are the branches. It is the branches that bear the fruit. The little foxes come and eat the fruit off the branches and thereby destroy the harvest. The little foxes are small animals but they can do major damage. Lack of honour is a little fox that does great damage and yet we do not stop to give it much thought. After all, it's the culture of today. It is evident all around us in our homes, at work, at church, in marriages.

Favour-blocker

Lack of honour acts like a repellent because when we practice it our favour doors begin to shut. Honour, on the other hand, acts like a magnet so when we practice it our favour doors begin to open. It is a favour-blocker and favour runs far from anyone who does not honour God or others. We often don't realise it, but lack of honour is often why our heavens are closed. It stems from familiarity, pride, presumption, disobedience and an unsurrendered heart. When we are not experiencing favour in life, it is usually the result of a person or a principle we have dishonoured. Obedience to God's principles releases the relevant favour to us and when we choose to dishonour those principles, it blocks that particular favour from manifesting in our lives. There are principles that govern eating, drinking, and self-control, and abiding by them releases good health, good standing and peace to us, while choosing to dishonour them will simply block their release. It is a principle of the Kingdom – we can never receive from what we do not honour. I pray that this Kingdom culture becomes a revelation in our hearts so it can become a reality in our lives.

Miracles flow where there is honour; miracles are blocked where there is dishonour

God Himself has no problem honouring people so why are we so prone to dishonour each other? John 12:26

(NKJV) says, 'If anyone serves Me, him My Father will honour.' Mark's gospel narrates two incidents about Jesus' ministry, one in Nazareth, where Jesus came from, and the other in Capernaum. We are told in Mark 6:1-6 that Jesus could do no major miracles in Nazareth because of their unbelief. What led to their unbelief? Familiarity. Isn't that the carpenter's son? Didn't we grow up with Him? Who does he think he is? Their lack of honour produced unbelief, which shut off the Holy Spirit's power. How many times are we guilty of that? In Mark 1:27-28, 33-34, we see that there was a completely different outcome when Jesus went to Capernaum. The people had questions too but they received Him gladly, honoured Him, and showed no familiarity and the result was many miracles. The Holy Spirit's power flowed in much healing and deliverance. These two accounts show us that honour releases the power of God while dishonour greatly hinders its expression.

God is so serious about the principle of honour that He gives several very specific instructions to us on whom to honour and we see that He leaves no one out. We are told in 1 Samuel 2:30 to honour God first then he in turn will honour us. In 1 Peter 2:17-18, we are to honour all men and we must honour the king.

Servants are to be submissive to their masters with all respect. In 1 Timothy 5:17, it says we must honour the church elders. We are told in 1 Timothy 6:1 to honour and respect those who are our employers. In 1 Timothy 5:3, we're told to honour widows, and in Leviticus 19:32 we are to honour the elderly. In 1 Peter 3:7 and in Ephesians 5:22 we are to honour our spouses and in 1 Corinthians 12:23-25 we are to honour the unseemly parts of the body. There are blessings when we obey Him and honour those He commands us to honour. Honour opens doors and lack of honour slams them shut. Honour is a seed that produces blessings and access.

Honour God

We are to honour God. We honour God when we reverence His presence, when we demonstrate excellence and obey His Word. We honour God when we give, when we love with His love, and when we honour people. In 1 Samuel 2: 30 (NKJV), it says, '… For those who honour me I will honour, and those who despise me shall be lightly esteemed.' Lack of honour not only grieves the Holy Spirit, but it also quenches Him. Ephesians 4: 30 (NLT) tells us, '… And do not bring sorrow to God's Holy Spirit by the way you live.'

When we dishonour the Holy Spirit, we will never experience His presence. Would you go somewhere people disregarded and dishonoured and ignored you? Even if you went, would you stay? Let us always be careful to honour the presence of the Lord.

Honour All Men

God calls us to honour all men and women for the simple fact that He chose to give them life. All people are precious to the Father; they are as valuable to Him as His son, Jesus. We are to honour the uniqueness of people, the fact that they can do tasks and jobs we cannot or will not do. We are to honour all people – not just those higher than us but also our subordinates and peers. Respecting and reaching out to someone in a lower position does not reduce us in any way. We are simply practicing humility and obeying the word of God. Honour is a lifestyle we must sustain if we want to see favour from God or man. Philippians 2:3 (NIV) instructs us to, 'Do nothing out of selfish ambition or vain conceit. Rather, in humility value others above yourselves.' We dishonour others by trivialising them and not prioritising what is important to them. We dishonour our friends by regularly turning up late to meet them. Within the body of Christ, we are commanded to honour every member, actually giving more abundant honour to the less "presentable" parts. In 1 Corinthians 12:23 (NKJV), we're taught, 'And those members of the body which we think to be less honourable, on these we bestow greater honour.' We cannot sincerely communicate the love of God if we do not show respect to the person we are speaking to. By showing them honour, we are telling that person that they are important to God and therefore important to us.

Honour pastors, men, and women of God

We must show double honour to those who rule well, especially those who teach us the Word. In 1 Timothy 5:17 (NKJV), it says, 'Let the elders who rule well be counted worthy of double honour, especially those who labour in the word and doctrine.' When we don't acknowledge and recognise the hand of God on the lives of our pastors and men and women of God, we dishonour God. When we dishonour God's delegated authority, we dishonour God. Honour is not just what you verbalise. It's in your body language, it's in your actions and non-actions. Honour is in what you prioritise and what you don't prioritise. In the same way, dishonour shows itself in our flippant comments, our presumption and our overfamiliarity with our leaders and authority figures. Every time we criticise the hand of God on someone, we are speaking against God. Anointing, miracles, prophecy, preaching – everything looks easy until you try it yourself. Some of us can't even show up to church on time yet we are never short of opinions on the sermon or the worship.

Such attitudes simply close the door to you receiving favour or any spiritual gifts from them – even when those leaders pray for you with all their hearts. It is simply a Kingdom principle. The people of Jesus' hometown did not honour Him, and Jesus called their lack of honour "unbelief". In other words, when we dishonour a man or woman of God, we shut down the power of God. Men and Women of God have paid the price for the anointing. People are not anointed by luck or at random, there is always a price they have paid. Some have made heavy sacrifices in order to serve God and that's the reason why, when you speak against them, even in secret, God punishes you in the open. Remember the story of Miriam and Aaron in Exodus 12. They spoke against Moses when he married an Ethiopian woman. Moses didn't even hear them but God did and the outcome was leprosy for Miriam. We must be careful of how we speak against our leaders even when they make mistakes. We ignore the following admonition at our cost. In 1 Chron 16:22 (NIV), it warns, 'Do not touch My anointed ones, and do My prophets no harm.' We will only receive from our leaders when we recognise, acknowledge, and celebrate the hand of God upon them. When we do not practise honour, we shut down the flow of God's power from them to us.

Honour our parents

Ephesians 6:2-3 (NKJV) says, 'Honour your father and mother (which is the first commandment with a promise), that it may be well with you and you may live long on the earth.' In Genesis 9:20-27, we read that Noah alone was considered by God Almighty to be blameless. Noah alone found favour with the Lord. Noah believed God and obeyed God's instructions to build the ark. He faithfully preached repentance for over one hundred years while building the ark, yet his words converted no one. Noah experienced the horrifying destruction of every man, woman, child, and animal outside the ark. Perhaps Noah was experiencing post-traumatic stress disorder, but after the flood, he made wine and got so drunk that he collapsed naked in his tent. The great man of God lay unconscious, drunk and naked. Ham, one of Noah's three sons, sees the shameful state his father was in and decides it would be funny to expose his father's nakedness. He tells his two brothers, who discreetly come and cover their father's shame, unlike Ham. Ham dishonoured his father by trying to expose his shame while Shem and Japheth honoured their father by covering his weakness. Ham had forgotten that the only reason he had not died in the flood was because of his father, Noah. When Noah woke up from his drunken stupor, he was still anointed. He knew instinctively which one of his sons had dishonoured him and pronounced a curse on him. I wonder how he knew. I bet it's because that wasn't the first time. He cursed Ham's son, Canaan. Why didn't Noah curse Ham instead? Noah knew that just as Ham had been to him, so Canaan would be to Ham. He said Canaan would be "a servant of servants" (see Genesis 9:25).

This story tells us that our own future and the future of our children are attached to how well we understand the value of honour and that a curse follows a dishonouring spirit. It is very difficult to obey this scripture when we have been treated very badly by our parents. All we can do is enlist the help of God, maintain certain boundaries where necessary, and choose to honour them and love them with the love of God. Whatever age we are, or our parents are, we are to honour them not just for their sakes, but for our own sakes too. We are to honour them whether they are good, bad, average or absent because parents give us access to earth.

Dishonour impacts our children

How we respond to the imperfections of our superiors determines not just our destinies but also the future of our children and our children's children. Whilst not everyone has children, most of us have younger people in our lives who look up to us in some way. Do they hear you constantly complain about your boss? Do they hear you criticise your pastor or the neighbours? What about when we voice our disdain of politicians, prime ministers, presidents, and leaders, or share derogatory things about them on social media? Do we ever stop to think that we are actually sowing wrong seeds, teaching our children how to *not* be successful in life? A dishonouring spirit is a licence for the devil to keep our children frustrated and stop them from being blessed and prosperous and yet the culture of the age calls authority-bashing freedom of expression. Children generally model their lives after their parents as they learn how to deal with the imperfections of life. As parents, we determine whether they will become rebellious and angry at authority figures or whether they will be free to relate to the imperfect authorities over them and still honour them.

Honour people in authority

Your boss, pastor, teacher and parents are all imperfect. If we can't learn to honour an imperfect leader, we will never advance in life because there are no perfect leaders. When we expose, humiliate, or dishonour our leaders by telling others of their weaknesses, we are actually short-circuiting God's favour on our lives. But when we honour their office, we can receive the benefit of that office in our lives. I prided myself on not being in awe of any authority figure and I was ready to take them on whenever I didn't agree with them. I don't think I was ever openly rude but I did love to challenge my teachers, parents, and bosses. Did I ever stop to think I was dishonouring my dad or a teacher with my forthrightness? I was more interested in scoring points or showing my friends that I was fearless until wisdom and adversity showed me that I was only hurting myself with this attitude. We will never advance in life with such an attitude. Again, it's easy to be deceived into thinking that God has adapted His Kingdom culture to suit the culture of this age but remember the God we serve says He never changes. Malachi 3:6 (NKJV) reminds us with these words: "For I am the LORD, I do not change…"

To be successful, we need to be able to submit to leaders who are imperfect without dishonouring them. 'But, if I do that, I will feel like a hypocrite, a "yes" man.' If you don't show honour, you are already being a hypocrite because a true Christian would esteem and respect people. We don't always have to trust people, but we must always honour them in obedience to the Word of God.

Sow seeds of honour

Lack of honour is a seed we are sowing. Every seed reproduces. We must be careful not to sow seeds whose harvest we are not ready for. I invite you to stop and listen out for what the Holy Spirit is saying to you. Is He highlighting an area where honour has been lacking? Is He convicting you of anything as you were reading? He reveals to redeem.

I invite you to pray this now and make things right before Him.

Father, thank You for this revelation you have given me about honour. I am truly sorry for not practising Kingdom culture by walking in honour towards You and towards all men and women. Forgive me and cleanse me of my sin by the blood of Jesus. I ask You to close every wrong door I have opened because of my dishonour. I ask that every door that has remained closed as a result of my dishonour be opened to me now. Please empower me to practice the Kingdom culture of honour. I make a choice to honour You always and to honour people, in my words, my actions, my body language and my attitude. In Jesus' name, Amen.

PART THREE
Becoming is not for quitters

THE REMAKING

Stripped!

The chrysalis is the stage in the caterpillar's journey when the "baby" tissues break down and the "adult" tissues form. In this stage, it is no longer a caterpillar but it is not yet a butterfly either. Unless it is willing to die to its caterpillar self, it cannot continue to become the butterfly it was born to be. Transformation will aways involve a form of death to self.

'Whenever the pot the potter was working on turned out badly, as sometimes happens when you are working with clay, the potter would simply start over and use the same clay to make another pot.' Jeremiah 18: 1-4 (MSG).

Life situations can force your identity to be changed overnight. A sudden bereavement can change you from a married man into a widower, a miscarriage can remove your label of expectant mum, and redundancy can change you from a high-flying executive into an unemployed jobseeker. Isaiah 43:1-2 (TPT) says, 'When you pass through the deep, stormy sea, you can count on me to be there with you. When you pass through raging rivers, you will not drown. When you walk through persecution like fiery flames, you will not be burned; the flames will not harm you.' This scripture indicates the inevitability of the storms of life by the use of the word "when". Our loving God allows these storms as part of His reforming process.

When the Potter starts His remaking, I can only describe the process as being stripped.

Identity crisis

We tend to define ourselves by our milestones and achievements and this becomes our identity. Whenever any of these are removed, we can go through an identity crisis. Who are you when you are no longer a mum or a dad? Who are you when you are no longer a teacher or a manager? Who are you when your promising football career is cut short by injury?

Suddenly I didn't know who I was. Where were all the props I had used to define myself, which gave me my identity and my security? Everything I defined myself by was gone - all my props were removed in one fell swoop.

Ruth, the businesswoman, who sat on various boards and got invited to speak at women in business events. GONE!

Ruth, the married Christian woman. DIVORCED!

Ruth, the generous person who helped others out of financial difficulty. BROKE!

Ruth, the healthy woman who had only been in hospital twice to have her children. SICK!

Ruth the confident, knowledgeable speaker. A NERVOUS WRECK!

I was facing what felt like hell in both my personal life and my business life. I'd always thought I was strong and had all the answers and here I was – without a clue as to what the future held. On top of that, I was having serious health problems and my doctor was threatening to fit me with a pacemaker! It was a scary place to be. I felt like a failure. A failure in business, a failure in marriage, and a failure as a Christian.

Jesus is in the boat with you

In the midst of all the crises and inner turmoil, I always felt that God was with me. I never once felt His disapproval. Instead, His presence grew even stronger. Considering what was going on in my life, I slept better than I had for years. There were times when I would literally feel the presence of someone with me in the house and I would turn around to see who it was but of course I didn't see anyone. The presence of God was very strong and very reassuring. He showed me that I was not alone and that He was with me. Whatever storm may have hit you, always remain assured that He will never ever leave you or forsake you. Listen out for His voice and His reassurance and comfort in the storm. Hebrews 13:5-6 (NKJV) says, 'For He Himself has said, "I will never leave you nor forsake you." So we may boldly say: "The Lord is my helper; I will not fear. What can man do to me?"'

Help always comes as we look to Him

Help comes in the form of people to comfort and encourage us. It comes in the form of practical resources we need. God will always provide the support you need and throw you lifelines to get you through the storm. Make sure you maintain an attitude of gratitude through the difficult seasons and appreciate those God sends to help you. My family rallied around me to support me and the girls with their love and generosity. They always seemed to know when to step in with a cash gift. Again, I could see the hand of God just saying, 'Ruth, I'm with you, I'll never leave you, I'll walk you through this.' My church family, particularly my pastors, were so supportive, they knew me well and knew my situation and never once judged me. They were very sensitive and supported me with love, friendship and prayer.

My business partner was more like a friend and a brother to me through thick and thin. He supported me with his friendship, and his contacts when I needed them and, above all, picked up all the slack that arose when I was in no fit state to do much. He never once said, 'Ruth, I do far more than you in this business so I ought to get paid more.' It was always equal and at times he would suggest that I have more as I was now a single parent. May the Lord Himself reward every single one of my helpers in their time of need.

There are lessons in the storm

Slowly I came to the realisation that my challenges were teaching me to depend on God and not on myself. I realised that, hard though it was, this was the love of God at work. I learnt that destiny fulfilment was never going to happen with the old version of Ruth who thought she knew it all, who felt showing vulnerability was weakness and that compassion was for wimps. God showed me His faithfulness in so many ways as

He systematically dismantled all the props I had used to build the version I was familiar with. I began to feel compassion for others who perhaps were in a difficult situation because of poor choices. The God we serve never deals with us as we deserve – so how could I be His follower and have a different outlook? I was becoming conformed to His image through the things I was suffering. Pride in my own abilities, my own skills, my own money, my own decisions were all fading away and being replaced by a new humility I had never possessed.

You know how some kids absolutely hate vegetables but we make them eat it anyway? Why? Because it's good for them. Well, I've always hated Brussels sprouts since I was a child so whenever I'm going through a difficult situation that I know God expects me to walk through, I call them my Brussels sprouts. I tell myself that I don't have to like them but I do have to eat them. My advice – eat your Brussels sprouts or whatever vegetable they represent in your life. Why? Because they are good for you. You don't have to like them but you do have to eat them in order to grow.

An identity crisis involves a very difficult season of not only being stripped but is also a time of great humbling and learning the power of humility. A time of turning from dependence on yourself to dependence on God. A time of seeing life from His perspective and not your narrow one. A time of shedding what you have become so that you can be reformed into who He really made you to be. Are you ready to view your challenges as a demonstration of the love of God and to see His pruning as a labour of love? Are you ready to change your perspective? Will you eat your sprouts?

Shame, shame, shame on you

Shame has a way of making you feel disqualified and inadequate. The feeling of being stripped can also bring with it a lot of feelings of shame. You may feel strange. You may feel kind of naked. You may feel exposed. You may feel like something is missing from you. You may feel as though everywhere you go people are talking about you and pointing the finger. I had such a strong sense of failure. There was a voice saying, *Ruth, you're such a failure.* You failed at marriage and you failed in business. Shame was building up. I felt I'd got it wrong because my marriage didn't work out. Perhaps I should have stuck it out. Several well-meaning people told me about how God hates divorce, and that translates into "you're in God's bad books".

After 16 years of marriage, I wasn't used to attending social functions on my own. Obviously, people also don't know what to do with you now that you are single and in a bid to avoid a situation where you are both at the function, neither of you gets invited. Even church socials posed a challenge for me, anything that involved couples reminded me that I was separated. I began to resort to just staying at home. The shame continued to build up. I went from loving to lift my hands high up in worship to not wanting to because I didn't want anyone looking at my "naked" ring finger. It felt weird when I was filling out forms and instead of ticking "married" now I had to tick "divorced". All I know is that I began to feel increasingly ashamed of my situation. All along a voice kept whispering in my head, reminding me of how I had messed up – marriage is for life and the Bible says God hates divorce. The voice kept saying that all those people were right and I should have stuck it out - no wonder my life was in such a mess.

Disqualified

I felt unqualified if I was asked to help out a couple who were having marriage problems and so I would make excuses. I'd failed at marriage so how could I possibly give advice on someone else's marriage? I felt ashamed because all my other siblings were still married and I wasn't. No one said anything, but I still felt like I had ruined the pattern and I'd let the side down. Why couldn't I just endure as so many other women do? I felt like I was no longer qualified to be a leader in my church because, with the exception of one person who was still single, all the other leaders were married, and I'd ruined that by not "enduring" my hell.

My business had all but failed and that was another source of shame for me. I had gone from being co-director of our own company, with 18 staff, to being on my own with two kids, a mortgage and almost no source of income. The day my mentor suggested going to apply for state benefits so that I could at least get some help with my mortgage, I felt sick at the thought. Where was my faith? Eventually, things got to a stage where it made sense for me to go and get some help. I felt that shame again! *Aha*, the voice said, *this is what it has come to – claiming unemployment benefit.* I mustered the courage to go and I went in and filled in the forms. I did qualify to claim while I tried to look for work and I got help with my council tax. My confidence was shattered, I didn't have the confidence to apply for any high-flying job so I tried applying for jobs I felt

I could do in my current state. I did get a few interviews but was always told that I was overqualified and they were curious as to why I was applying. It was like I couldn't even get a job, so I felt even more shame. I finally found some freelance work providing bookkeeping services but even that didn't last very long as the company was experiencing serious cash flow problems. I had to go and sign on for unemployment benefit every fortnight and on my way there I would be thinking, *what if someone I know sees me going in? Lord, this is embarrassing for me – can't you fix this?* It was like nothing I tried to do worked and a voice kept saying, *Shame, shame, shame on you, Ruth.*

Perhaps you're going through a tough situation that has brought with it feelings of shame or being disqualified. A season like I have just described brings its own pain but you must learn to view it as an essential part of being reformed. God uses such seasons to deconstruct any pride you have in your achievements, status, who you are, your abilities, in material possessions, or your connections. It is a season of dying a very needful death and it can be very painful. In order to be able to become a butterfly, the caterpillar has to fall apart completely, decompose down to its very essence and be devoid of any shape or consciousness. It literally dies.

There is nothing left of it. Saying goodbye to the old you, who is being systematically killed off, is tough. It is also challenging to see that anything good can be done with what remains. Some days it can feel like nothing is left, except this unrecognisable alien. Little do you know that you are simply shedding the things that don't belong at the new level where He is taking you. John 15:2 (NKJV) says, 'Every branch in me that does not bear fruit He takes away, and every branch that bears fruit He prunes, that it may bear more fruit.' A pruned rose bush looks totally butchered to the untrained eye. Pruning is never pleasant but pruning is necessary for fruitfulness. God is at work as He prunes us, working on our heart attitudes and conforming us into the image of Christ.

Counting it all joy

God loves us too much to leave us the way we are. It is the Lord who weaves the tapestry of our lives. We can only see it from the wrong side but God can see the beautiful picture He is producing. We see a woven tapestry from its underside with knots and messy strings, but once it is turned over, there is this beautiful picture with lots of different colours in a beautiful setting. I believe the knots relate to the pruning, unpleasant but so necessary for increased fruitfulness. Ephesians 2:10 (NKJV) puts it this way: 'For we are His workmanship, created in Christ Jesus for good works, which God prepared beforehand that we should walk in them.' God, the master craftsman, is at work in our trials and in our adversity. This is why James 1:2–4 (NKJV) appeals to us: 'My brethren, count it all joy when you fall into various trials, knowing that the testing of your faith produces patience. But let patience have its perfect work, that you may be perfect and complete, lacking nothing.'

What is joyful about trials you might ask? What is joyful about feeling embarrassed and ashamed? What is joyful about not being able to pay your bills? What is joyful about feeling judged and misjudged? We count it joy because of what we know. We count it joy because we know the one we have believed is in complete control. We count it joy because of knowing what the trials will produce in us. We count it joy because of the end product. Something good will always come out of your season of pain – *if you let it*.

In any season of great challenge, whatever form it takes for you, know that God is at work transforming the caterpillar into a beautiful butterfly. The butterfly represents beauty and freedom. And fruitfulness awaits because, as the butterfly feeds on nectar, it also pollinates, causing fruitfulness.

DON'T WASTE YOUR PAIN

Don't waste your pain

Have you noticed how we never forget the lessons we learn the hard way? Have you ever found yourself in an impossible situation that doesn't seem to end and it looks like there is no light at the end of the tunnel? You've tried all the things you know to do and yet nothing changes. Or things actually get worse. Those situations where it seems like God is deaf to your cries, your prayers, and your tantrums. Yes, this God who is so good and this God who answers everyone else's prayers but is not answering your desperate prayers. When it seems like the God who answers by fire doesn't seem to even want to light a candle on your behalf. This may resonate with some people while others may be saying, 'What on earth is she on about?'

If you've been there you have got the battle scars to show for it and if you're in the middle of it, just hang in there even if it is literally by your fingernails. If you have no idea what I mean, and you are a believer who is seeking to mature then one day you will. I found out that there's simply no way of avoiding this element of God's processing. Tests and trials are part of His process of transforming you. I have learned that the only way to truly know God is through adversity and pain. It takes many forms and everyone's adversity is unique to them. Between life, the devil, and ourselves, things happen that are unpleasant. Situations arise that we feel shouldn't have happened or at least not to us. Trials come that we feel this mighty all-powerful God of ours could fix in a moment and yet doesn't.

God, where are you?

Life often hurts. The road of adversity is full of bumps, twists and turns. It's a lonely road. You don't know when it will end. Many times, you want to just give up because it seems like there's no point in carrying on. Nothing changes for the better. Everyone has a testimony except you. The new year comes and goes while you keep carrying over your prayer topics from the previous year. Awesome prophetic words you have received remain unfulfilled. Did they get it wrong? Did I not war enough with my prophecies? Is God a respecter of persons after all? If we haven't known who we have believed, the doubts begin to set in. It is a time of great confusion, much questioning, frustration and loneliness. A time of asking, 'Why? Why me? What did I do? Where did I go wrong? God, where are you?'

It could be a long wait for a child – while the biological clock ticks away, miscarriage after miscarriage, operation after operation.

It could be the loss of a beloved child, or a beloved spouse, or a beloved parent.

It could be the loss we experience through separation and divorce.

Or the loss of a job followed by a prolonged period of unemployment and the resultant financial and self-esteem woes.

It could be a business venture that spectacularly failed.

It could be a devastating diagnosis of a life-threatening illness.

It could be a tragic accident that leaves us incapacitated and no longer able to work.

Or you could even be hit with a combination of several such scenarios.

I could go on and on. It's enough to say that no one gets to skip the storms of life.

Job 5:7 (NIV) points out, 'Yet man is born to trouble as surely as sparks fly upward.' When the troubles of life seem to be totally overwhelming, remember that God will not allow you to go through more than you can bear. Whatever you may be experiencing is actually common to man, others have been through similar situations. In 1 Corinthians 10:13 (MSG), it says, 'No test or temptation that comes your way is beyond the course of what others have had to face. All you need to remember is that God will never let you down; He'll never let you be pushed past your limit; He'll always be there to help you come through it.' This reminds us of the faithfulness of our God and tells us that all the while He has His watchful eye on us to make sure that it never gets beyond what we can bear. It's like a parent taking their child for a vaccination. It is painful for the child and for the parent to see the child in pain but he knows how necessary it is for the child to go through with it. The child may look at the parent reproachfully through their tears wondering how on earth Mum or Dad could allow them to go through this. In the same way, sometimes we blame God for not rescuing us from the situation. The inclination is to withdraw from Him instead of drawing even closer. Or we decide it is the enemy and pray many prayers binding the devil.

I even resorted to sometimes attending a prophetic prayer meeting in the hope that I would receive some kind of prophetic word or direction. I was desperate for anything that would shed some light on my situation, but each time there was either no word for me or a wonderful word about how God would use me in ministry. There was nothing whatsoever to do with my current very practical challenges. At that time, I didn't want to do any ministry, I felt I needed ministry myself!

God is the same yesterday, today and forever

Eventually, it began to dawn on me that the God I serve is indeed the same yesterday, today and forever. God never changes, if He was good before my life fell apart, then He is still good even though my life is falling apart. If God was good in 2012 then God is good in 2018 and onwards. If God was good before my marriage failed then God is still good now that it has failed. God is good irrespective of whether my life sucks or not. I learnt to separate my view of Him from the nature of my circumstances because who He is and His credentials had no connection whatsoever to whatever I was going through. This realisation really helped me to be able to begin to praise and worship Him in the midst of difficult circumstances.

Even though you may be experiencing a season of great confusion and pain, reminding yourself that God does not change will stop you from secretly blaming Him in your heart for your challenging circumstances. It stops you from sinking into a spiral of self-pity or hopelessness. Focusing on God's unchangeability means you can leave the road called "God is mean because my life sucks" and find the road called "God is always good irrespective of what is going on in my life".

Picture God seated on His throne in heaven – omnipresent, omniscient, "omni" everything. If you know Him and spend enough time with Him, then you know without a shadow of doubt that God is good. Though you may not understand, you know that He is your good, good Father and that He loves you beyond anything you could ever know. Here is your heavenly Father, all-good, all-knowing, all-powerful, and all-loving, who isn't doing anything whatsoever to change this difficult situation. There could only be one reason for His not doing anything about it – He is up to something that will eventually benefit you. You can rest assured in that knowledge of Him. You must begin to recognise that there has to be a bigger reason for what is going on than what you can see from your perspective.

Ask God to give you His perspective on your situation, to help you see the same thing from His panoramic all-knowing viewpoint rather than your very limited one. Our heavenly Father derives no joy whatsoever from seeing His children hurt. If He willingly made the ultimate sacrifice for us when we weren't looking for Him, then for Him not to move on our behalf could only mean that there is a very good reason for the perceived lack of activity. I guess the operative word is *trust*. We must choose to trust Him in our circumstances and not question His love for us because of those circumstances. Instead of leaning on our own understanding, we should learn to trust Him with the things we don't understand because we know His credentials and His integrity – He truly is a good, good Father. He tells us in, Proverbs 3:5-6 (NKJV), to, 'Trust in the Lord with all your heart and lean not on your own understanding. In all your ways acknowledge Him and He shall direct your paths.'

Boot camp

When I was going through my difficult season, the phrase I coined was "internal work for eternal purposes". When God is doing internal work for eternal purposes, He is not particularly interested in whether we are comfortable or not. I had a daily battle fighting the voice of self-pity but, thankfully, with His help,

I managed to stay afloat and never succumbed completely. I would simply try to get His perspective on the matter and this helped me immensely until I finally came to the realisation that I was enrolled in God's training school and my job was to study hard and pass the course. The subjects were humility, compassion, obedience, kindness, self-control, forgiveness, perseverance, and trust. These are tough subjects and you don't get to pass them by just reading a book on the topic – you have to do the practical work of walking it out in order to pass. Galatians 5:22-23 (NKJV) says, 'But the fruit of the Spirit is love, joy, peace, longsuffering, kindness, goodness, faithfulness, gentleness, self-control. Against such there is no law.'

No one learns perseverance just from reading a book on the topic – we learn perseverance by persevering through challenges. Unlike the gifts of the Spirit, which we receive freely, the fruit of the Spirit is not received freely, it is developed over time as we walk through our tests and trials. We develop the fruit of love by having to learn to love difficult people. We develop self-control as we learn to stop reacting in situations and, rather, be more measured by responding instead of reacting. God will take each of us through His training school as part of His remaking process, arranging and rearranging circumstances as tests which we must pass in order to develop the fruit of the Spirit in us.

Adversity, the great tutor

Throughout the training season, I was learning to play to the audience of one. To care about what the Lord thought of me rather than what other people thought. Several times, I would ask the Lord how I was doing on the course. I felt His pleasure and I stopped looking for a change in my circumstances and instead I would say. 'Lord, if you're happy then I'm happy.'

I'll never forget one morning when I asked Him how I was doing on His training course and I distinctly heard Him reply, 'You got a C.' I said, 'Oh no, I've never had a C on any course in my life'.

To me, a C is a "you just scraped through" kind of pass, i.e., I passed but only just. Straightaway, He brought to my mind a situation where He had asked me to forgive someone who had hurt me and though I did forgive them, it had taken me a few weeks to obey and forgive.

During that time, one evening at our weekly small group meeting, my leader was praying over each of us and when she got to me, she said, 'You keep asking the Lord how you are doing on the course. He says to tell you that you are doing great.'

I burst out laughing. I thought, *God, you really have such a sense of humour.* Of course, I'd never told her or anyone else about this "course" or how I would often ask Him how I was doing. It was in this rather lengthy season of great challenge that I can honestly say with all sincerity that I grew more in that five-year period of challenge than I had in the previous 25 years. Adversity truly is a great tutor – if you allow it. It's your choice.

Don't miss the hidden treasure

Somewhere in the midst of any horror and pain is a treasure and to miss discovering that treasure is a complete waste of that pain! The more I understood the season I was going through, the more I determined not to waste a single ounce of my pain. Since the adversity is happening anyway, it would be tragic not to gain anything from it except pain. Always make sure you don't miss any of the treasure hidden within the difficult circumstances you are going through. Since you are going through it anyway, it would be a shame to go through such painful circumstances and not have gained something precious of eternal value in the process.

My advice – don't waste your pain. Not a single drop of it. Recognise it as one of the pieces in the puzzle of your life. Don't try to explain your life by a piece in the puzzle because you can't see the full picture in the one piece. But when you take that piece and fit it in with all the other pieces then you begin to understand why it was necessary for that awful thing to happen in your life for the full picture to form. Whatever you do – don't waste your pain.

If you are determined not to waste any of your pain then join me as we pray: *Father, it's been tough and it seems unending but I come before You in faith knowing that You are working in me both to will and to do Your good pleasure. Help me to maintain the right heart attitude, even during these difficult circumstances I am going through. I choose to keep trusting You and I receive strength to persevere and press through. None of this pain will be wasted because I know that somehow You will work it all out for my good. In Jesus' name, Amen.*

PROCESS – GOD'S QUALITY CONTROL MECHANISM

Process

Different callings and issues call for different processing and testing. No one can avoid going through process in preparation for their calling. Process is defined as a system of operations which produce an end result. Or, to quote my dear mentor and friend, 'It is the process that produces the person that possesses the promise.' If Jesus didn't get to skip process, I don't see how any of us can and yet expect to fulfil destiny. God knows exactly what is required to bring about His purposes in us and just in case we think it's all the devil, let us take a look at a few people in the Bible who went through processing.

In Genesis 37-50, we read how Joseph had to grow into the destiny that God had for him and how he stepped into it well-prepared and well-seasoned only after many years of great adversity. People say that Joseph's mistake was telling his brothers about his dreams but if he hadn't how would he have ended up in Egypt and eventually save a whole nation? What the brothers meant for ill, God turned around for good. It's called process.

In the book of Exodus, Moses spent a whole heap of years in hiding in Midian before he took up his role as the deliverer of Israel. This deliverer was 40 years in the making. And then he spent another 40 years with the Israelites wandering in the desert. And then we are told in Numbers 12:23 that he was the meekest man that ever lived. It's called process.

There is an 18-year gap in the life of Jesus when all we are told in Luke 2:40 is, 'And' the boy grew and increased in favour before God and man'. It's called process.

David gets anointed by Samuel to be king of Israel and then we read in 1 Samuel 21-23 about how he has to spend years in hiding and running away from King Saul, who is trying to kill him. David only became king about 15 years later. It's called process.

All of these Bible heroes had a lengthy and challenging period before seeing their promises fulfilled. Is it that God needs more time to do what He has said? Does He enjoy keeping us waiting and waiting and even watching us grow old? Why doesn't He do things more quickly? Or is there a much loftier reason for the apparent delays and challenges? In order to fulfil destiny, you cannot dodge going through the school of process. It is His quality control mechanism to make sure that we are fit for purpose. Process is generally not pleasant, but God isn't that interested in your comfort during your processing. Process is an essential part of God's transformation system and the purpose of this process of transformation is for fulfilling the destiny that awaits you.

I have a few questions for you:

Has God given you some promises which haven't been fulfilled yet?

Does it sometimes feel like nothing is happening and life is passing you by?

Do you feel like everything that can go wrong in your life has gone wrong?

Does it seem like God is completely silent in your case while it's all happening for other people?

If the answer is yes, then you're being processed in God's school of transformation.

People who have been through can help bring others through

You can't speed up the process. You can't take a shortcut because any "do-it-yourself" attempts to help

God always lead to disaster. We read in Genesis 16 about what happened when Abraham and Sarah decided to help God speed up the fulfilment of His promise to them. When it comes to process, fasting doesn't work and neither does crying. And as for murmuring and complaining, they only serve to lengthen the processing period even more. We read in the book of Exodus about the Israelites in the wilderness and how a journey of roughly 11 days took 40 years! The period between the call or the promise and its fulfilment is called process. We can't escape or dodge the process if we are going to fulfil our destinies. Our true ministry comes out of the things we've been through. God uses people who have been through to help bring others through because we know how it feels, we have been there, and we have come out. Process transforms us. Process makes us authentic. Process gives us staying power.

God's refinery

Refining gold or silver requires intense heat. The season of adversity brings us to the place of transformation and to be transformed we must go through the refiner's fire. During Bible times, the silver refiner would place the silver in a metal container over the hottest possible fire. As the silver began to melt and bubble in the heat, the dross, scum, and impurities would rise to the surface and be skimmed off. The process of skimming continued until there were no more impurities left in the silver. The proof that the silver was fully purified was that when the refiner looked on the surface of the silver, they could see their own face properly mirrored in the silver.

The prophet, Malachi, tells us in Malachi 3:3 (NKJV), 'He will sit as a refiner and a purifier of silver; He will purify the sons of Levi, and purge them as gold and silver, that they may offer to the Lord an offering in righteousness.' God tests us the same way as a silver refiner refines silver. In other words, God uses heat in the form of trials and pressure to perfect His work in us. Jesus, our high priest, went through the refinery. In Matthew 4:1, we read how Jesus was driven (compelled, sent, led) by the Spirit into the wilderness. In Hebrews 5:8, the Bible tells us that, even though Jesus was God's Son, He learned obedience from the things He suffered. We are not to be surprised when we face a fiery trial. 1 Peter 4:12 tells us that we should not think it strange: 'Concerning the fiery trial which is to try you, as though some strange thing happened unto you.' In 2 Corinthians 4:17, apostle Paul calls trials our momentary light afflictions and says they are working for us a far more exceeding and eternal weight of glory.

God will test us, in the furnace of affliction, to remove impurities from our hearts. The hotter the furnace, the more the impurities are brought to the surface. God graciously skims them off and He continues with that skimmer until He sees His own image reflected in our lives. The process of refining is complete when He can see His reflection in us and that is when He takes us out of the furnace. It seems the gentler modes of His love are less effective at bringing about transformation than the tougher ones. Our flesh is stubborn, and our hearts are naturally wicked. But there is great comfort in this promise in Isaiah 43:2 (NIV): 'When you walk through the fire, you will not be burned; the flames will not set you ablaze.'

We will encounter fiery situations, but our consolation is that the fire will not destroy us. Our loving God uses adversity, trials and tests of different kinds. And through it all, He is sitting on His throne and yet He is also right there with you. His eye is on the clock and His hand is on the thermostat. He is sitting as a refiner when all hell seems to break loose, when you lose your job, or your best friend betrays you, your business fails, the husband they prophesied hasn't shown up, healing is slow to come, or your ministry is shrinking instead of growing. He is right there with you. Recognise that He really is the fourth man with you in the furnace of fire. Trouble consumes our impurities – the dross and the chaff – and ultimately makes us useful in the Kingdom. It makes us a vessel of honour, worthy of the master's use. Nobody refines clay but gold and silver must always be refined because refining metal requires intense heat.

If you are currently in the refinery, don't be discouraged by the heat of the process. Instead cooperate with the refining and be encouraged knowing that it only lasts as long as necessary. At the end, you will emerge a vessel of honour. Once refined, you might sometimes lose your shine but a quick polish always brings it back. What is produced in us is for eternity and we never have to endure that particular fire again.

The wilderness season

When circumstances refuse to change, then it's time to change the questions we ask God, from "why" to "what". Have you ever prayed and asked God for a word and all you ever got was silence? Have you prayed, fasted, and declared the word and nothing about your circumstances has changed, maybe things even ended up much worse? This period is often referred to as the wilderness. It can feel like God has taken a sabbatical. It can feel like you are on your own in a thick, dark forest and there's no one else there but you. You don't know where you're going, you can't see where you are going, and you're plain scared.

It took a while, but eventually, in my wilderness season, I learned to quieten myself and change the questions I was asking God. I learned that it was pretty foolish to be angry with the only person who could help me. It is the devil who uses life situations to paint God incorrectly in our eyes. He knows that the moment we are in doubt about God's faithfulness, or His Father's heart towards us, then we cannot trust God. We begin to doubt that He will come through for us. We begin to blame Him for our circumstances when all along it is Satan who has orchestrated them. We must settle it once and for all that God is always good and He does not have a split personality either. Anytime this same good and kind God does not rescue us out of very difficult circumstances then it can only be because He is up to something that is for our good. We must have the patience and trust to wait for it to unfold.

We must reach a place where we stop linking our dire circumstances to the character and credentials of God and His intentions towards us. When we recognise that God is at work in the dark forest of our lives, we can then start to cooperate with what He is doing and not miss the treasure He has for us in the wilderness. Right there in whatever awful situation you are in, your Father is working something within you – internal work for eternal purposes. He is working some things out of you that don't belong inside you and He is working some things into you that are missing. Throughout the Bible, we see that not one person who started *and* finished well got to skip this aspect. Not even Jesus Himself. He learnt obedience through the things He suffered.

I don't know what seemingly unending or impossible circumstances you are going through right now. I don't know if you feel like you are in a really dark forest and can't seem to find your way out but the one thing I do know is this: God is *always* good. Don't ever allow the enemy to use your situation to redefine who God is to you. Refuse to allow him to discredit God or change His credentials. He truly is the same yesterday, today, and forever. He is good whatever your circumstances look like, and you will come through this – if you do not faint. Make a very deliberate choice to trust God, especially when you don't understand or agree with Him. Accept that part of the official way to know Him is through adversity and pain. Determine that you will find every hidden treasure in that difficult season of preparation as you cooperate with Him Through all that pain you are becoming who you are meant to be. Don't let a single drop of your pain go to waste.

Whatever you do, don't go below sea level

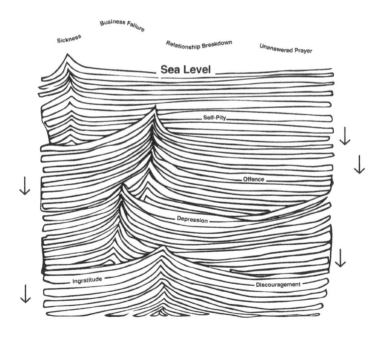

Testing seasons can drive us "below sea level". In other words, this is when life's circumstances make us feel down, overwhelmed, and like we cannot go on. Life has a way of throwing major curveballs. It could be a life-threatening diagnosis, a sudden death of a loved one, job loss, or marital breakdown. All of these things are significant events which we are rarely prepared for.

When we are in the midst of difficult circumstances, life can feel almost surreal, like a movie, except you're in it. When everything that could go wrong in my life went wrong all at once, there were many times when I felt like I couldn't cope. I wanted to give up. I hoped it was just a nightmare that I would wake up from and find it wasn't true. For days on end, self-pity would engulf me and all I would do was cry. All kinds of questions would go through my mind. How could all this be happening to me? Wasn't I God's favourite daughter? Why was I going through so much misjudgement, betrayal, health problems, and financial problems? I didn't like my life one bit and could see no way out of where I was. I would imagine the negative circumstances as waves, pushing me below a point where coming back up to the surface would be extremely difficult. It felt like I was drowning in a sea of impossible realities. Somehow, as I kept crying out to God for help, I managed to stay just above sea level or to quickly drag myself back up when I was going down. In that period, I learnt that the further below sea level I allowed myself to go, the longer and more difficult the journey back up was.

Imagine all the sensations we experience once we are below sea level. Breathing becomes more difficult and seeing becomes more difficult. Our perspective is distorted when we are below sea level and we become even more overwhelmed and therefore less able to cope. When you are under the sea, no one can see you to help you and you can no longer shout for help. It's difficult to keep fighting when we can no longer breathe. We only get weaker and weaker due to lack of oxygen and then we begin to swallow water which further incapacitates us until there is no more fight left – we give up.

We are not designed for living below sea level, there's no oxygen there for us. Life below sea level suffocates us and eventually drowns our joy, our peace, our perspective, our gratitude and even our love for God as we silently blame Him for our negative circumstances. Living below sea level is a sign that we are wallowing in self-pity. So, whenever you find yourself heading down there, literally drag yourself back up by a deliberate act of your will. Don't listen to your feelings or your thoughts – use your will to come back up because the alternative is too costly.

I feel sorry for me

Sometimes our story or the situation we are in can feel like it is the worst ever. We feel that our challenge is unique and that no one could possibly understand what we are going through. We can feel that no one can go through so much and survive.

'Look, even I feel sorry for me,' I said to my dear friend who was doing her best to try and lift my spirits. I had recently heard about all sorts of untruths being circulated about me.

My precious "reputation" was being torn to shreds with lies and I expected God to say, 'There, there, Ruth.' Instead, He immediately reminded me that He often got very bad press too. I knew He was right and that shut me up, but it was hard to shift the feelings of self-pity that had taken hold of me. He was trying to stop me from going below sea level while I wanted to have a pity party.

Self-pity feels good but it is not of faith.

Self-pity is self-absorption.

Self-pity has a loud voice, and it keeps on speaking if we don't stop it in its tracks.

Self-pity speaks unbelief by pandering to our emotions and our wrong thinking.

Self-pity makes us the instrument the enemy uses to destroy us. It is self-destruction.

Self-pity says, God, you don't know what you are doing.

Self-pity says we don't trust God anymore.

Self-pity says that God does not work all things together for our good.

Self-pity keeps us preoccupied with ourselves.

We must take control of our thought lives. As the saying goes, you can't stop the birds from flying over your head, but you can stop them from nesting there. Philippians 4:8 (NIV) urges us, 'Finally, brothers and sisters, whatever is true, whatever is noble, whatever is right, whatever is pure, whatever is lovely, whatever is admirable – if anything is excellent or praiseworthy – think about such things.'

According to this scripture, some of our thoughts are illegal. It's that simple. We shouldn't be thinking any illegal thoughts. Evaluate the thoughts going on in your head. Are they pure, lovely, and praiseworthy? If not then they are illegal, so stop thinking them. Period. We need to think on the right things and then speak the right things to ourselves. The just shall live by faith, not self-pity and without faith, it is impossible to please God. Refuse to drown in self-pity. We actually do have a choice and we always have the power to choose correctly. We have the power to bring ourselves back up from below. We have the power to choose to change our thoughts from dark ones to good ones. We have the power to choose to take our thoughts captive and make them line up with the Word of God. We have the power to choose to disagree with the words of the enemy.

Let's exercise our power right now.

Declare with me –

I refuse to drown in self-pity. I declare that God will cause every negative circumstance to work out for my good. I choose to change my attitude from being a victim to being a victor. I choose to reject negative thoughts and I choose to think thoughts that are lovely and pure and of a good report. Amen!

Painkillers

Pain will always seek an outlet and keep seeking an outlet until healing comes. Stuff happens and life can be hard. Sometimes we get more than we bargained for, so we look for our own painkillers, or coping mechanisms, to help us get through the day and deaden the pain. As we invent these painkillers, we often end up in different kinds of addictive behaviour patterns. We try all sorts of things with one sole objective – to numb the pain. These include isolation, comfort eating, shopping, hoarding and self-neglect. We can also develop anxiety, phobias, or become overly dependent on prescription drugs to function. I could go on and on. Pain is usually hiding underneath all these behaviours.

My painkiller was clothes shopping. Ever since I was a little girl, I loved to dress up. I always had an eye for nice clothes, especially bright colours and how to put them together nicely. Although it never got so out of hand that I got myself into debt, I saw myself go from just having a love for nice clothes into – let's face it – an addiction. I did it because I felt they made me happy. As it progressed, I would buy clothes and not even take them out of the shopping bags. When I ran out of wardrobe space, I would shove the bags in the kids' wardrobes and put some in the spare room's wardrobe. I would give some of them away as gifts and convince myself that my shopping wasn't getting out of hand as I was also being a blessing to others. When one of my junior staff once observed to me that she had never seen me wear the same outfit twice, I told her that couldn't possibly be true and to watch her mouth. My pastor once threatened to come home and look in my wardrobe to see where I was storing all my clothes and, of course, I discouraged him! This was my own way of making myself happy.

Looking back, the saddest part was that the Holy Spirit Himself would always speak to me about it when I was about to make yet another purchase. I would literally hear Him say, 'Ruth, you don't really need this.' I would reply that it didn't cost much and remind Him that I was very unhappy and this made me happy. Even though money was tight, because I wasn't getting into debt, somehow I felt it was all right. What's wrong with a little bit of happiness given my challenging circumstances? I never considered that I was in disobedience to the Holy Spirit or that I was being a poor steward of the resources the Lord had given to me.

Clutter

Like all addictions, my painkiller was a quick fix at best – I would feel good briefly and then that feel-good feeling would lift and then I would need another fix. Instead, my out of hand clothes shopping created another problem for me. It led to clutter, clutter, and more clutter. I didn't get into debt but what I got into was clutter – big time. Clutter of any kind is a sign of a cluttered inside. Something was desperately wrong inside and I was using clothes shopping to try to fill that void, which wasn't really working. It was a long journey out of that place of addiction because no one really saw it. If I was rapidly putting on weight from overeating or showing signs of becoming addicted to alcohol or to prescription drugs, someone would have noticed. But it's not easy to spot addictive shopping because it is not physically external (beyond someone noticing that you don't often wear the same thing twice or them looking in your wardrobe). Before long, it became easier to wear something new than to go through my overflowing wardrobe or myriad suitcases to find an old outfit. I knew it had become a problem but I was deeply unhappy and I felt this was one thing that I enjoyed and that genuinely made me happy.

The devil knows what weakness to exploit in us. I can say no to chocolate so he wasn't about to tempt me to go overboard with chocolate. I have always been pretty disciplined when it comes to food generally so he knew he wouldn't succeed in getting me to comfort eat. But he knew that my weakness was for nice clothes, especially at a bargain price, so that is what he exploited. I never thought that I was grieving the Holy Spirit or that it was poor stewardship. I was a tither and good giver so why couldn't I do what I wanted with some of the rest? I wasn't doing anything irresponsible. The clothes I bought weren't expensive. I had all sorts of justifications I would give as to why I could continue with my behaviour. All the while my home was getting more and more cluttered.

I did try to stop – several times. I would fast, set myself a budget, and not go to the shops at all for a while – you name it, I tried it. But, lo and behold, as the season of deep unhappiness and turmoil continued, I would find myself back shopping for more clothes I didn't need. And I just didn't want to talk to Holy Spirit about this one area. Why didn't He want me to at least have some fun?

Surrender the habit

As I continued on my healing journey, I learned to look to Him more and more to fill the void and to heal my pain and not use clothes shopping as my fix. Without a doubt it was also an issue of surrender. I was refusing to surrender that part of me to Him. When I began to understand more about surrendering all of me to Him, I was able to surrender even this addictive behaviour to Him. Instead of trying to stop shopping, I surrendered it to Him. He was so gracious and simply said to me one day, 'Ruth we will go shopping together.' Now when I want to buy something, I involve Him and if I sense He doesn't think it's a good idea, we don't go shopping. Online or otherwise.

It was important that I did a complete clear-out. I had to clear out the stuff I was holding on to, both material and internal to get rid of it all. I had to clear my mind of all the rubbish in there too. I gave a whole heap of my clothes away, got rid of some more by giving them to charity and now most of the clutter is gone and it is so much easier to tidy up my wardrobe. I can enjoy my bedroom because I don't have clothes stored everywhere. I no longer have a void that I use shopping to fill because I have allowed God to deal with my pain at its root and heal me.

I've shared my painkiller with you to show you that any of us can get into all kinds of unhelpful behaviours when we are struggling and going through a lot of pain, by looking to ourselves instead of looking to Him. I shared this because, chances are, there is someone reading or someone you know who is battling with pain and also using some form of painkiller in a bid to get rid of the pain. What is the behaviour pattern that you know has gone completely out of hand? What is it really covering up or compensating for? What is it trying to fix? Only one person can give you a permanent fix and His name is Jesus. Only Jesus can take away the pain.

Will you simply surrender that painkiller to Him?

Let us pray. *Lord, thank You for highlighting this addictive behaviour pattern to me. I repent for using it as a fix for my pain and I ask You to please forgive me. I choose to give it up now, I surrender the habit to You and ask that You come and deal with the root cause. Please come and heal me of every pain and trauma that has led me to seek relief through this habit. I ask You to fill every void that I have tried to fill with the wrong things. Thank You, Lord, for complete healing, in Jesus' name. Amen.*

Digging deep after loss

Losing someone or something you love is devastating, whatever the cause. Whether it is through bereavement, from a relationship or friendship that broke down, or one that did not materialise – it's all loss. At such times we have to dig really deep to find the will and the inner strength to carry on and be able to say, 'Devil, I may be down now but I'm not out.' The psalmist put it this way in Ps 30:5 (NKJV), 'Weeping may endure for a night, but joy comes in the morning.'

It's not over until God says it's over. Joel 3:10 (NKJV) says, 'Let the weak say I am strong.' We have to engage our will to choose our response, and to find the inner strength to make the right choices and decisions. We have to use our will to choose to trust when we don't understand. To choose to get out of bed when we would rather stay and not face life out there. We can use our will to choose to watch over our health, our thought life, or juggle work and parenting on our own. The list is endless. In every situation we face, we have the power to use our will to override our emotions.

Do I really have to? Yes, you do – for destiny's sake. You cannot become who you are meant to be from underneath your duvet. When Jesus faced the toughest time of His life in the garden of Gethsemane, He prayed this prayer in Luke 22:42 -43 (NIV): '"Father, if You are willing, take this cup from Me. Yet not My will, but Yours be done." Then an angel from heaven appeared to Him and strengthened Him.' No doubt Jesus was in great agony and wished He did not have to go through with what was ahead. He expressed His wish that the "cup" be taken away and then He immediately submitted His will under the will of God. 'Not my will but yours be done.' We are told that an angel from heaven came and strengthened Him.

There is a lesson to be learned here. If God won't change or avert a situation, then He will always send us the help we need to strengthen us for what lies ahead. We don't have to like our circumstances, and there's nothing wrong with crying out to God to change them, but we must submit our will under the will of God, just as Jesus did. We too must say, 'Nevertheless, not my will but yours be done.' God says that He will never ever leave us nor forsake us and He also says that He will not let us go through more than we can bear. When we go through the difficult places, God will always send us the strength we need to go through. There is grace available for each part of the journey. Dig deep for the strength to choose right.

Just pray this prayer and say …

Father, I thank You because, like Job said, You know the way that I take and when You have tested me I shall come out as pure gold. Thank You for the strength to dig deep and submit my will under Your will. Let Your will be done in my life. I receive strength to go through this season knowing that at the end of it I will be a vessel that You can use for Your glory. In Jesus' name, Amen.

BECOMING FIT FOR PURPOSE

Are you fit for your purpose?

In 1 Corinthians 6:19 (NKJV), we're asked, 'Or do you not know that your body is the temple of the Holy Spirit who is in you, whom you have from God, and you are not your own?' How many of us stop to think that this scripture makes us responsible for what we put into our bodies and how we care for and maintain it? We take such good care of our church buildings. our homes, and our cars. We must equally take good care of our bodies because that is where the Holy Spirit lives; one way we look after our temple is by looking after our health.

A time comes when you realise that you absolutely must include a fitness regime in your lifestyle. It could be because you are getting older or had a health scare, but we must reach a point where we no longer make excuses and continue to ignore any lack of fitness. In my case, it was a combination of getting older and recognising that I didn't do any exercise beyond walking to and from my car, which was usually parked outside the house, the car park at work, church, or the supermarket! That meant I was lucky if I was clocking 5000 steps a day!

My wake-up call was the result of an incident at Heathrow Airport. My pastor and I were travelling abroad to a conference. We checked in early and then sat somewhere near the boarding gate to enjoy a leisurely coffee while we waited. After some time, we checked the screen to see if it was time to start boarding. We took a look and – guess what – the boarding gate had been changed from Gate 10 to something like Gate 42! The new boarding gate was a good 20-minute walk away from where we were sitting and, to make matters worse, the message on the screen said "gate closing"! In short, walking wasn't going to cut it! Now my pastor is extremely fit and runs eight miles every day. Then there's Ruth who runs zero miles every day and only walks to and from her car. She turns to me and says, 'We're going to have to run. You're okay to run, aren't you?' Of course, I said yes – we had a flight to catch. We took off and, oh, how I ran my little heart out. We made it in time but I assure you it took my heart at least 30 minutes before it could stop thumping madly and beat normally. They then decided to delay the flight in order to allow all those who had been messed up by the gate change to still get onto the flight. In other words, we could have walked the 20 minutes and still made it!

It was a wake-up call for me because it was clear that I simply was not fit. I made a mental note to address this when I got back. I wasn't looking for anything particularly strenuous to do so I decided to start walking. Walking was easy and I did it a few times a week but found it rather lonely, so I began to ask God to give me a walking partner. I had no idea where one would come from. I attempted jogging but it was hard. My heart would start beating so hard I thought that I was about to die! I didn't give up and, slowly but surely, I could run a bit further and further until I could jog up to two miles without having to stop. All this time I continued praying for a walking partner. I prayed for two years for someone to walk with. One day, a good friend from church said to me, out of the blue, 'Ruth, why don't we go walking together?'

I replied, 'But how can we when you live at least two miles away from me?'

Her answer was, 'Don't worry, I will drive over to you and then we can go for our walk.'

We began walking a few times a week, sometimes for hours if it was a weekend, and it was the beginning of a much closer friendship and bond which has lasted until today. We are gym partners and more like sisters than friends. Who said God isn't in the business of answering our prayers and giving us more than we ask or imagine?

Free training in perseverance

After about a year I wanted to add to the walking and running short distances routine as they were becoming rather tame. There was a young man at our church who was a very good personal trainer so I asked him if he would come over to my house and teach me a few exercises I could do from home. I was expecting him to show me a few simple exercises I could do using a dining chair or the sofa. He duly arrived one Saturday afternoon and I ended up being given a one-hour training session, at the end of which he said, 'OK, see you same time next Saturday.' I was so tired I could hardly speak. He showed up again the following Saturday with all sorts of mean-looking equipment for another one-hour session. After our third Saturday session, I was convinced he was trying to kill me. All of it was hard and everything hurt. I thanked him for all his help and explained that I couldn't afford whatever it is that personal trainers charge so we would have to end the sessions. When I asked how much I owed for the three sessions, you'll never guess his reply. 'Don't worry about paying me, it's a seed I'm sowing into your life! And I'm going to keep coming every Saturday if you're up for it.'

God was definitely up to something! First, He gave me a walking partner and now He had just given me a personal trainer who was giving up his Saturday afternoons to come to my home to train me for free. He was very anointed with it too and would often pray over my bad back while training me. I made up my mind to make the most of this God sent opportunity and I viewed it as my training in perseverance. Let's face it, no one ever got fit from reading a book, the only way to get fit is by pushing past the pain. I persevered and slowly the one-hour session did not feel like forever and I no longer hurt all over. As I persevered, I noticed my long-standing back pain improved and I could once more stand for hours if I needed to without any pain. The best part was that I could spend hours in the garden and plant all my colourful summer plants, which I loved to do, and my garden began to look lovely again.

Heathrow Boarding Gate 42 here I come – running! I have maintained my fitness efforts and I'm pleased to say I am probably fitter than a lot of ladies my age. I can't say I wake up and actually look forward to going to the gym but I don't let that stop me. I simply tell myself that I am becoming fit in order to fulfil my purpose. I choose to use the training as my opportunity to keep growing in perseverance and endurance and to see it as my way of caring for my temple where the Holy Ghost lives.

Keep fit for your purpose

Our bodies are vessels. They are containers. When we don't do our part in making sure the container is fit for purpose, it can get compromised and give up on us altogether. This can happen irrespective of the container's contents. Can you imagine all that anointing you carry not being used because the container broke? We owe it to ourselves to stay fit in order to fulfil our purpose in full.

I am doing my best to make sure I am fit for my purpose. When I fall by the wayside, I get back up and start again. How about you? Are you serious about being fit for purpose? Or have you assumed that because you are zealous for God, and so busy doing things for Him, He will somehow take away the responsibility from you? He is not going to, God always leaves us our part to do. If you are already keeping fit for your purpose – good on you. Your container will thank you and so will the Holy Spirit who lives there. And if you need a wake-up call like I did then let's speak to God about it right now.

Just tell Him that you recognise that this is an area that needs attention and ask for His help to find what fitness regime works for you, then get started. And please stick with it, not because it's easy but because your purpose is calling, because you refuse to allow the container to fail you and above all because the Holy Spirit lives there.

I gave my sugar to Jesus

Do you have a sweet tooth? I must confess I like to have dessert after my meal. A meal is not complete without something sweet after, even if you reduce it to a couple of rich tea biscuits… OK, maybe three!

I love all kinds of teas so the hardest thing with addressing my sweet tooth was having sugar with my tea. I never considered the fact that if I had five cups of tea in a day that was ten spoons of sugar a day. These things add up in your body!

For a number of years, I had sensed that the Lord was speaking to me about cutting back on the sugar in my tea. I wasn't overweight or experiencing any health issues, but that sense wouldn't go away. I did try but I would invariably revert to two sugars or not drink the tea at all. My solution was to reduce the number of cups of tea I had in a day instead, to a maximum of two.

One January, after completing my first Daniel fast, I really sensed that I needed to address the sugar in my tea issue. That morning, as I reached for the sugar to add to my cup of tea, for some reason I began to think about Jesus and the price He paid for me on the cross. I thought to myself, *Jesus did all that for me, surely I can give Him my sugar as a sacrifice.* So I just said out loud, 'Jesus, you died on the cross for me so I give you my sugar.'

I went ahead and made my first-ever cup of tea without sugar! I didn't like it at all but I had already given my sugar to Jesus so I had no option but to persevere. My taste buds struggled to conform to the new tea reality and many times I only managed half a cup, but I refused to go back to having sugar in my tea. I had given it to Jesus – period. My taste buds would simply have to catch up with my decision and they eventually did. I have no idea why He told me to check my sugar intake but I'm glad I was able to obey with His help. Who knows – perhaps there was a future health issue that has been avoided. God doesn't always elaborate when He gives us an instruction, but I do know that it pays to obey. As the prophet Samuel said to Saul in 1 Samuel 15:22 (NKJV), 'To obey is better than sacrifice.'

How many of us Christians think it's wrong to drink alcohol, yet overeat or stuff our faces with the wrong food and think that's okay? We think it will never affect our health, after all, by His stripes we were healed. For some of us, it might be fizzy drinks – that can of coke you absolutely must have. It could be half a packet of chocolate chip cookies or that bottle of red wine you have when you're feeling stressed. If you sense that the Lord is speaking to you to cut back or stop a certain food or drink altogether, it's a warning you should heed. He knows something we don't know and He doesn't want our container to give up on us or our temple to suffer ill health.

It is always our responsibility to take care of our temple, not God's. Your body is simply a container and if you don't take care of the container, it can limit you regardless of all your zeal and passion for the things of God. As the saying goes, prevention is better than cure. I always add that it is also much cheaper in terms of pain avoided as well as money and resources spent. God is merciful but we must not abuse His mercy by living irresponsibly.

PART FOUR
Emerging unrecognisable

REFORMED

Formed again in a different form

Metamorphosis is the process by which the caterpillar transforms into a butterfly. After it is reformed, the caterpillar bears no resemblance whatsoever to its new self, the butterfly. The butterfly is better, faster, moves on a higher plane, and, above all, is more useful than the caterpillar ever was. To reform simply means to form again. When a person is reformed it means they are created again after a period during which they existed in a different form. This is God's plan for us as we are carefully and lovingly processed on the wheel by the hands of the Potter.

The Message Bible expresses it beautifully when it talks about God's original plan in conforming us to the image of Christ, His first born and our big brother. Romans 8:29 (MSG) says, 'God knew what He was doing from the very beginning. He decided from the outset to shape the lives of those who love him along the same lines as the life of His Son. The Son stands first in the line of humanity He restored. We see the original and intended shape of our lives there in Him. After God made that decision of what His children should be like, He followed it up by calling people by name. After He called them by name, He set them on a solid basis with himself. And then, after getting them established, He stayed with them to the end, gloriously completing what He had begun.'

The outcome of our transformation is that God can now use us in our reformed state. We are no longer novices; we have proven experience. We have experienced life with all its ups and downs and emerged better, stronger and wiser. We have tasted and seen that the Lord is good. We haven't just believed by receiving Christ into our hearts, we know who we have believed and we are persuaded about who He is, His integrity and His ability. We have encountered Him personally, on the mountain top and in the valley. Our knowledge of Him is experiential and not just theoretical. He has tried us and tested us in the fire and we have come out as gold, a vessel worthy of the Master's use. We don't just bear His name but can be sent out on Kingdom business as true ambassadors for Christ.

Use your practising certificate

Your destiny incorporates your pain. God will use us in the very area where we have experienced our greatest agony. Our personal experiences give us our testimony and make our words and ministry to others more compelling. It is the very things we've been through that prepare us to be a blessing in someone else's life in the very area in which we have experience. A practicing certificate is a licence to practice a particular profession and proven experience is how you get your practicing certificate. Just as a qualified solicitor or accountant needs proven experience in order to provide their services to the public, we also need proven experience in order to minister to others with compassion and love. If your heart is to create a successful business empire in order to finance the work of the Kingdom, then God will allow you to taste what it is like to have no money. A powerful healing ministry will usually involve you battling and overcoming a serious illness too.

God will always make sure that you have a personal connection to your call so that you know what it feels like to be in the shoes of those you are called to. That's your practising certificate. Don't despise your challenges – use them. Hebrews 5:8 (NKJV) says about Jesus, 'Though He was a Son, yet He learned obedience by the things which He suffered.' Jesus went through false accusation, being misunderstood, rejection, criticism, ridicule, controversy, mockery and hatred. I'm sure that the gossip about Mary and her "so-called" immaculate conception reared its head again and again while Jesus was growing up. Think about the impact that would have had on Him.

Hebrews 4:15 (NKJV) says, 'For we do not have a High Priest who cannot sympathise with our weaknesses, but was in all points tempted as we are, yet without sin.' Why did Jesus have to suffer all these things? It was so that He could be a high priest who was touched by the feeling of our infirmities. A high priest who knew how we feel from His own experiences because He had acquired His practising certificate.

One morning, I was listening to a message by Joyce Meyer where she mentioned her abusive past and how God had healed her so completely that it required real effort to even remember that season of her life. She went on to explain that she was having to recall it in order to share her testimony at a battered women's refuge. I started to think about how horrific her life must have been growing up and started asking the Lord some questions. 'Lord, why didn't you rescue Joyce when her father was abusing her? She was young and defenceless – couldn't you have rescued her? I know she's healed now but couldn't it have been avoided in the first place?'

I heard the Lord say to me, 'I didn't just come to earth to die and be raised back to life. Part of the reason I came to earth was to taste your lives. There is no pain in heaven. I came to live your lives so that I would not be a phoney high priest.' Then He continued, 'Part of the reason you are going through all this is so that when you speak no one will say, "What does she know?"' I never got any answers to my questions about Joyce Meyer. He simply spoke to me about my life and I realised that this experience, however unpleasant, meant I was walking in the shoes of many of the people I would one day be speaking to.

Our pain produces empathy and we need compassion and empathy to minister effectively to others. People can sense the difference between empathy and sympathy. They can sense whether you have a practising certificate or not. Sympathy is us being moved by the pain of others but with no point of reference. Our pain gives us a point of reference. Jesus didn't pray for Peter not to deny Him, or not to lie or swear, He prayed that his faith might not fail. Luke 22:32 (NLT) says, "But I have pleaded in prayer for you, Simon, that your faith should not fail. So, when you have repented and turned to me again, strengthen your brothers." After this experience, Peter would be able to empathise with those who were struggling with their faith because his own faith had been shaky before.

There are times when God will see you walking right into a situation and not rescue you from it. Why would

He do that? So that when you come out of it you can be the one to strengthen others who find themselves in similar situations. You will be the best person to help people out of that particular kind of situation because you've been there and come out of it. In 2 Corinthians 1:4 (NIV), it says, 'Who comforts us in all our troubles, so that we can comfort those in any trouble with the comfort we ourselves receive from God.'

How much of what you have been through are you using to help others? The best child bereavement counsellor is the one who has also experienced the loss of a child and been able to overcome the trauma and pain of that loss. That's how you make the devil pay – when you use your practising certificate in the area of your greatest pain. That's how you make him regret sending that arrow your way. Let's poke the devil in his eye, right where it hurts.

So, go on – dust off your practicing certificates and use them for God's glory.

No surrender

When we give our lives to Christ we step into the river of God. We all start our spiritual walk at the shallow end, but God will always challenge us to go deeper, to progress to the point where we have no option except to swim. It doesn't matter where we are at, He always has more for us, further for us to travel, wider for us to explore and deeper for us to go. Psalm 42:7 (NKJV) says, 'Deep calls unto deep…' He brings us through the waters at a certain pace as we choose to yield to Him. The reason? So that we can bring His healing to a hurting world. So that we can reflect Christ everywhere we go. So that the people out there can experience Christ through us.

I was at a morning session at a church conference where the speaker shared her story about adopting and bringing up a child who had several challenges, including severe autism. She shared about the sacrifices involved, the things she had to lay down, including a successful ministry she loved, in order to devote her time exclusively to bringing up her child. It was heart-piercing and, at the end, she invited anyone who was willing to come to the altar and surrender everything to God. Tears were rolling down my cheeks as I did my best to remain composed. I did not want to go to the altar and present myself for more breaking, pruning or whatever this wonderful lady was inviting us for. Somehow my legs moved and carried me there because

I found myself at the altar. As I knelt there, I had a strong sensation of standing in a pool, in quite deep but with my feet still firmly on the floor. Then I felt that my feet were no longer on the floor of the pool and I began to feel like I was floating. And then the Lord spoke to me from Ezekiel 47 about the river. He told me that though I was in the river, I always wanted to make sure that my feet could touch the floor, or should I say the riverbed. It was very vivid and He asked if I was finally willing to let go and swim in the river. I was a bit scared because I can't swim, but He was right there with me so I said yes as the tears kept flowing. There are different depths in our relationship with God. The Holy Spirit, our guide, leads us through each level but it is up to us to choose how far and how deep we will go with Him.

Ankle-deep – Ezekiel 47:3 (NKJV) says, 'And when the man went out to the east with the line in His hand, he measured one thousand cubits, and he brought me through the waters; the water came up to my ankles.' We all start at ankle-deep level – the water is up to our ankles, and it's pretty refreshing and relaxing. We roll up our trousers and get our feet wet. We splash around a bit enjoying the water running against our feet. No pressure. Prayers get answered quickly. We are more into the things of the world than into the things of the Spirit. Most of "us" is still on display. The water is shallow and so is our experience of the river. Our testimonies consist of, 'I couldn't find my keys and I prayed and, guess what, there they were, on the dining table! Yay!' Children play in shallow water. We are baby believers, drinking milk, not yet able to eat meat. We are not yet able to be salt and light to those around us. There is definitely a time and place for this while we are getting to know Him, but we must not remain in the shallow waters for too long. Shallow water makes shallow Christians. There is no real commitment involved. You can turn back anytime and walk back to the shore. You are in your comfort zone and loving it. Self is very much on display at this level, nearly all of you is visible. You are still in charge of your life; your life is very much your own. But don't park here, there's so much more.

Knee-deep – Ezekiel 47: vs 4a (NKJV) says, 'Again he measured one thousand and brought me through the waters; the water came up to my knees.' From ankle-deep level, He brings us through the waters and now the water is up to our knees. We're getting wetter and we're progressing in the things of God. We're developing a strong prayer life, learning to lean on Him and trust Him more so we venture a bit further forward and deeper in the things of God. We have a pretty good degree of commitment, but movement is still somewhat easy. You start to feel the power and the current of the river but you are still standing on your own two feet in the water. You are well within your comfort zone and most of you is still very visible. You are not ready to give up certain habits and attitudes. You care more about what people think about you than what God thinks. You are not yet willing to go deeper into the unknown realm of what God has for you. It's still about you, your abilities, position, and education. You are still in control. Self is still very evident at this level. Don't park here either, you have only just begun.

Partial surrender

Waist-deep – Ezekiel 47: vs 4b (NKJV) continues, 'Again he measured one thousand and brought me through; the water came up to my waist.' He measures another 1000 cubits and brings us through the water and now it's up to our waist. Now you can really feel the current of the river, it's getting rather scary, especially if you can't swim. Movement is more difficult, and you are more wet. The current can push you forward if it's strong. About 50% of you is still visible in the river. God is controlling more of you, but you can still change direction if you choose. Your feet are still firmly on the riverbed. You can still walk; you can still turn back. Do you leave your comfort zone, or do you stay? You are passionate and willing to serve but only if it's convenient. You are obedient but not always immediately. You are still the one in control. You are trusting God, but there is a "Plan B" just in case. You are committed, but you have a bagful of excuses. Committed but with a break clause.

Committed – yes, but, sorry, I forgot I was on the rota.

Committed – of course, but I couldn't make it on time for worship practice.

Committed – absolutely, but I just can't do evangelism, it's not my thing.

Committed but comfortable.

Wet in some parts and dry in others, half-wet and half-dry, struggling to give my everything. Surrendered but not fully. It's a kind of crossroads – *do I give everything to God or not?* This is the level where the Holy Spirit is dealing with your inner self. Dealing with the things that He sees but you don't. The areas of your life that need changing – sinful areas, unforgiveness, pride, greed, and selfishness. Things that the devil can use to trip you up along the way, like wrong priorities, attitudes, and behaviours. Many of us choose to park here because we still want to be in control.

Why is it so difficult to relinquish control? What stops us from getting wet all over? Why do we still have a Plan B? Why won't we let our feet get off the riverbed? What is it we are afraid He will ask us to give up? What sacrifices are we holding back on making? Fear of the unknown, fear of the opinions of people, and lack of trust all contribute to our reluctance to surrender completely. We're afraid God might ask for more than we are willing to give Him. We are not ready for full commitment. We are afraid of the price or the sacrifice that may be involved. We are afraid to let self die totally. We are not yet ready to die. Self is still evident at the ankle, knee, and waist levels. He does not want us to remain at these levels because there is so much more. Deep calls unto deep, so we cannot fulfil our purpose hanging about in shallow waters.

I stayed parked at this level for a very long time. I knew I had come a long way from not wanting to even dip my toe in the water to going ankle-deep, then knee-deep, and now waist-deep. I was happy where I was,

I could still feel the riverbed where my feet were firmly planted. It was safe, it was comfortable for me. I was happy where I had settled. I was serving faithfully, doing more ministry stuff, and venturing out of my comfort zone on occasion. However, God always expects us to go beyond standing and wading to start swimming in the river. He wants us to let go, relinquish control, and trust Him to take over in full because destiny is fulfilled at the level where there is no turning back. That morning, as I knelt at the altar and I could no longer feel my feet on the floor of the pool, I finally said yes completely to Him. I was ready to swim, to let the Holy Spirit take over, withholding nothing from Him.

Total surrender

Water in which one must swim – Ezekiel 47: vs 5 (NKJV) says, 'Again he measured one thousand, and it was a river that I could not cross; for the water was too deep, water in which one must swim, a river that could not be crossed.' When we get to this level our feet can no longer touch the riverbed. It is not possible to stand anymore. You can't stand, you can't walk, and it is not easy to turn back. The water has gone above your shoulders and the only way is forward. The only way is to swim and you have to be carried along by the river. Every part of you is wet, the water has covered everywhere. You're in so deep, you have no option but to let it carry you. The river is in control and dictates where you go and not you. This is the place of "not my will but yours be done". It is the end of self and self-effort. You have left your comfort zone completely. This is the place where you hand over full control to Him. You obey God regardless of whether it is comfortable or not, whether you might look stupid or not. The people standing on the riverbank can no longer see you standing in the water, all they see is the river flowing. All they see is the Christ in you, not you. You live by faith in Him, you know His voice, and you obey His voice, the voice of another you do not hear. You are led by the Spirit and not by your own desires. This is the place of total commitment and total trust in Him. The place of total surrender to His will and His direction.

The water has to be in you to flow out of you. John 7:38 (NKJV) says, 'He who believes in Me, as the Scripture has said, out of his belly will flow rivers of living water.' You must be totally submerged in the river and follow its flow to the people who are hurting, sick, or fearful. This requires trust, humility, and the total surrendering of your life into God's hands. It requires death – death to self. This is how Apostle Paul described it in Galatians 2:20 (NKJV): 'I have been crucified with Christ; it is no longer I who live but Christ who lives in me.'

Your progress in the river depends on how far you will allow the Holy Spirit to work in your life. On how much you will let go and let His will be done in your life. On how much you will decrease so that He can increase. At each level, you surrender more of your self-will to God. At each level more of self dies until you are fully submerged and carried by the water.

Fruitfulness

The beautiful result of our total submersion and surrender is fruitfulness and healing. Ezekiel 47:6-9 (NKJV) says, 'Then he brought me and returned me to the bank of the river. When I returned, there, along the bank of the river, were very many trees on one side and the other. Then he said to me: "This water flows toward the eastern region, goes down into the valley, and enters the sea. When it reaches the sea, its waters are healed. And it shall be that every living thing that moves, wherever the rivers go, will live. There will be a very great multitude of fish, because these waters go there; for they will be healed, and everything will live wherever the river goes."' This describes how we become those whose very lives bring healing to others. We bring hope, we bring joy, we bring peace, and wherever we go there is fruitfulness.

Let us pause here and pray: *Father, whatever level I am in the river, today I choose to go deeper. I choose to surrender my all to You, holding nothing back. I want to move from ankle-deep to knee-deep. I want to move from knee-deep to waist-deep. I want to go to the level where I have to swim in the river so that I can bring Your light and hope to others. Thank you, Lord. Amen.*

PUTTING ON HUMILITY

Humility – the way up is down

In the Kingdom of God there is only one way up and that way is down. This is totally contrary to our nature and the world we live in. Humility is for those who want to go up in God's lift. In the Kingdom of God you go down in order to go up, you give to receive, and you die to live. God's will for our lives will always lead us on the pathway of humility. Matthew 20:26-28 (NKJV) says, 'Yet it shall not be so among you; but whoever desires to become great among you, let him be your servant. And whoever desires to be first among you, let him be your slave – just as the Son of Man did not come to be served, but to serve, and to give His life a ransom for many.' In God's Kingdom the way to become great is by being a servant. Whoever wants to be first should go even lower and be a slave to the people they want to be named first among. The greater your desire to be great in the Kingdom, the lower you must go to serve others and be empty of self. There are no exceptions. The taller the tree, the deeper the roots if the tree is to remain standing in a storm. The taller the building, the deeper the foundation must be for the structure to be secure. It's funny how trees know this principle, builders know this principle, yet many of us believers do not practice this Kingdom principle.

The only way to promotion with God is via the path of humility.

Humility is the result of being reformed in the Potter's hands. Humility is evidence that we are conforming to the image of Jesus. Humility is accepting that He is the Potter and you are the clay and that the clay does not tell the Potter what to make or how to make it. Isaiah 45:9 (NLT) expresses it very strongly when it says, 'Does a clay pot argue with its maker? Does the clay dispute with the one who shapes it, saying, "Stop, you're doing it wrong!" Does the pot exclaim, "How clumsy can you be?"' Humility is when you surrender self because you recognise that it has no ability or effectiveness whatsoever in the Kingdom. Instead, create room for Him to fill you to overflowing to touch the lives of others with His goodness, power, healing, and love. Humility says I am most useful to Him as an empty vessel therefore I empty myself of self and let Him be all in me. Humility is our willingness to truly surrender all and withhold nothing from Him for the sake of the Kingdom. This could be our plans, our time, money, relationships, and anything else He may require us to lay down, whether temporarily or permanently. Humility is giving up the need to be right all the time and win every argument. Humility is a lifestyle choice you make continually by an act of your will. Humility says He must increase, and I must decrease.

The opposite of pride is humility. Pride hides in the heart and then creeps up on you unawares. Pride strikes at every level. We can keep fighting it with the best of intentions, but we can never be free from it. The only way to conquer pride is by replacing it with humility.

It was during my journey out of the land of pride that I came across a book called *Humility* by Andrew Murray. God had taught me about the dangers of pride and how much it offends him. Prolonged adversity had worked a lot of pride out of me and then in His mercy the Lord took it a step further to teach me a better way. The book gave me a wonderful perspective on why I needed to be a nobody. I needed to be a nobody so that God could be everything in me. I learnt how to sink into my nothingness on many levels and slowly I began to notice dramatic changes in my responses to various life situations. I learnt that the emptier I was, the fuller I could be of Him. The more I got rid of self, which had nothing useful to offer, the more of Him I could carry. To empty myself of what is a hindrance to me so that I can make room for what is infinitely more useful and effective was a no-brainer, but it doesn't mean it was always easy. Humility took on a whole new meaning for me and I began to seek opportunities to practise it.

Humility is not going around being apologetic in life, saying please with every sentence and letting everyone walk all over you. You could be doing all that and be full of pride in your heart. Humility is simply the place of total dependence on God and total surrender to Him. The place where we surrender all to our creator God and allow Him to be everything. The place where we deliberately and continuously deny self by saying no to self! The place where we keep our vessels empty, clean, and clear so that He can fill us and flow through us to others. Jesus invites us to learn His secret in Matthew 11:29 (NIV) when He says, 'Take my yoke upon you and learn from me, for I am gentle and humble in heart.' Humility was one of Jesus' success secrets. Jesus said in John 5:30 (NKJV), 'I can of Myself do nothing.' Jesus said He only did what He saw the Father do. Jesus didn't do His own thing and then ask the Father to bless it. Humility is stopping to ask the Father where He wants us to go and going there in obedience, even if it is not where we want to go or had planned to be.

Say no to yourself

Humility is saying no to myself. Luke 9:23 (NIV) says, 'Then He said to them all: "Whoever wants to be my disciple must deny themselves and take up their cross daily and follow me."' To deny self is to say no to self before God. To deny self means admitting that self is of no value except as an empty vessel for God to fill. Pride exalts self, humility denies self, and therefore kills pride. When we deny self then God will lift us up. Luke 14:11 (NKJV) says, 'For whoever exalts himself will be humbled, and he who humbles himself will be exalted.'

As long as we are full of self, there is no room for Him to fill us, to do anything in or through us. If we are half full of self, there is only room for a half-filling. If we are one third full of self, there is only room for two thirds filling. But if we are completely empty of self then there is room for a 100% infilling. This is when we become more and more like Christ, when others see Him through us. All that oozes out of us is Christ and we exhibit His love, His power, and His anointing.

Do it yourself – you humble yourself, don't let Him have to do it for you. James 4:10 (NKJV) tells us,

'Humble yourselves in the sight of the Lord, and He will lift you up.' If you do not humble yourself, He will have to do it for you. We practice humility by being teachable, by trusting the Father, and by being ready to lay aside every weight of prejudice and preconception we have. It is so much easier to humble yourself than when He has to step in and do it for you. Each one of us has a choice to make between humbling ourselves or being humbled. The latter is usually very unpleasant.

Humility is having a sense of gratitude not entitlement

Humility means we come to God on His terms and serve Him on His terms if we want to achieve any success in His kingdom. God initiates and we respond. We don't initiate and then ask Him to bless it. We practice humility by always being thankful. Humility is when we recognise that the password for entry into His presence is "thank you" and not "gimme, gimme, gimme". When we do not have a sense of entitlement, there is always a reason to bless the Lord at all times and for His praise to be continually in our mouth. God tells us in Isaiah 57:15 (NKJV), 'I dwell in the high and holy place, with him who has a contrite and humble spirit.' The humble are guaranteed God's continued presence with them.

When I am weak, then I am strong

If self-humbling is the way up in the Kingdom, then we must be pleased to go through trials and tests because of the end result. The less we rely on our own ability, the more we draw on His ability. Paul had learnt this and says, in 2 Corinthians 12:9-10 (NKJV), 'And He said to me, "My grace is sufficient for you, for My strength is made perfect in weakness." Therefore, most gladly I will rather boast in my infirmities, that the power of Christ may rest upon me. Therefore, I take pleasure in infirmities, in reproaches, in needs, in persecutions, in distresses, for Christ's sake. For when I am weak, then I am strong.' The happenings in our lives that shame us, put us down, embarrass us, or belittle us, serve to strip us of self- importance and make us less proud and more humble. The more we recognise that of our own selves we can do nothing, the more we will depend on the Holy Spirit. This is why we must decrease – He is not trying to take from us, it is rather so that He can increase within us. We decrease in order to make room for Him.

Dress right – wear humility like a cloak

We must wear humility like a cloak. It's something we have to wear intentionally whenever we are interacting with others. In 1 Peter 5:5 (NKJV), it says 'Yes, all of you be submissive to one another, and be clothed with humility, for, "God resists the proud, but gives grace to the humble."' We must wear the cloak of humility so that we can carry the weight of His glory. If we have asked to carry His glory and if we are going to be able to bear the weight of His glory, then we must wear the cloak of humility. As we continue to humble ourselves, any leftover pride will be broken off of us. When God looks down at us, He looks straight into our hearts. He sees our motives; He sees what people don't see. Jeremiah 17:10 (NKJV) says, 'I, the Lord, search the heart, I test the mind, even to give every man according to His ways, according to the fruit of His doings.' It's important that we regularly ask Him to search our hearts to show us anything there that is not right or clean or pure in His sight. We are often so preoccupied with externals yet everything that God looks at and measures us by is internal.

We are dressed right when:

We think the best of others.

We give others the benefit of the doubt.

We don't lap it up when people compliment us.

We show kindness.

We are merciful.

We are not judgemental.

We are keenly aware of our own nothingness before God.

We put no trust in our abilities, achievements, or possessions.

We acknowledge each day that anything we have or do is only by the grace of God.

We can rejoice when others are blessed.

We do not think of ourselves more highly than we should.

We know we are just a nobody carrying a somebody.

How do we wear the cloak of humility in daily life?

We do this by saying no to self and what it wants, thinks, or wills. As far as we are concerned, self is bankrupt and has nothing of value to offer. We do this by giving the word of God top priority in our thoughts, in our words, and in our actions.

Now here is a scenario for you. You are upset with a friend, or a sibling, over something awful they did to you. You have every reason to refuse to contact them while you wait for them to realise their folly and contact you to grovel. Love says, *Why don't you let it go and give them a call anyway?* Self says, *Why should I? They are the one who wronged me and so they should be calling me to apologise. Plus, this is not the first time they've done this!*

There is a constant tussle between self and love – who is going to win? Practicing humility will cause us to make God's choice and His choice is always love because He is love. You wear the cloak of humility by saying no to self and yes to love – you call the person and show them God's love. Love is not proud and love keeps no record of wrongs, love is kind. We must say, 'Lord, I know what I want to do but I choose to say no to myself.' We must choose to sink into our nothingness and do what He would want us to do. In the toughest moment of His life, Jesus said no to himself when He said, 'Nevertheless not my will but yours be done.'

How many of us are walking in offence and unforgiveness without giving any thought that it is wrong and prideful?

It takes humility to forgive a wrong and reach out in love instead.

It takes humility to let go of a wrong and trust God to vindicate us in His own way and time.

It takes humility to feel like a complete fool but obey God anyway.

It takes humility to walk away from conflict, to choose the way of peace and not strife.

It takes humility to ask for feedback and face the truth about the feedback you receive.

It takes humility to point the finger at yourself and not everyone else.

It takes humility to admit that there isn't something wrong with everyone else and accept that I am the one who needs to change.

Humility means we lay aside our image

There are times in life when we will have to make a choice between maintaining our image or receiving our breakthrough. In the story about Naaman the leper, in 2 Kings 5:9-14, we see that he had to learn to humble himself in order to experience his miracle. Naaman eventually made the right choice, did as the prophet instructed, and was healed of leprosy. Humility means when He asks us to, we can lay aside our qualifications, position, wealth, skills, and accomplishments because, according to Isaiah 64:6, even on our best day they are all just filthy rags before the Lord. Every ounce of pride in us is systematically being killed off as we continue to practise humility.

I must know who I am

Before you can truly practice humility, you must know who you are. You have to know who you are and you need to have a strong sense of purpose. You have to be secure in yourself in order to be humble. You have to be strong to humble yourself and take a back seat. Unless we settle this within ourselves, we will struggle to serve others and struggle to serve Him. We will sometimes think that being humble will detract from us. You have to be able to declare with certainty, 'I am not my own. I have been bought with a price, a great price. I have been adopted into the family of the Most High. I belong, I am part of the family of the King, the servant King, which means I am a servant prince/princess. I am who I am because of the blood price that was paid for me. I serve others from the place of knowing that I am a prince and a king. I serve wearing my royal robes because I have nothing to prove to anyone.'

We must have the right perspective on humbling ourselves so that He can touch lives through us. Otherwise, we will not appreciate the need to empty ourselves of all that is self. We will continue to believe that self has value and continue to struggle to be nothing. Jesus was perfectly secure in the love of the Father and He was perfectly secure in His identity as a son. He knew the key to inheriting the earth and seeing God. Jesus knew that it was only through total submission and dependence that His mission on this earth would be accomplished, and, as a result, He could humble Himself, even to point of the worst possible kind of death.

Humility obtained Jesus the name that is above every name

Jesus obtained the name above every other name by taking the very nature of a servant, by being made in human likeness and by being found in appearance as a man. He humbled Himself by becoming obedient to death, even death on a cross. Philippians 2:6-7 (NIV) says, 'Who, being in very nature God, did not consider equality with God something to be used to His own advantage; rather, He made himself nothing by taking the very nature of a servant, being made in human likeness.' Jesus humbled Himself by letting go of His God nature, power, and privileges by making Himself nothing. Jesus emptied Himself of self so that God's healing and deliverance power could flow through Him to multitudes. He made many statements expressing His humility. In Mark 10:45 (NKJV), He said, 'For even the Son of Man did not come to be served, but to serve, and to give His life a ransom for many.'

In John 5:30 (NKJV), He said, 'I can of Myself do nothing … I do not seek My own will but the will of the Father who sent Me.' Because of Christ's willingness to become nothing, God gave Him the name that is above every other name. Christ's reward came as a result of His humility. Philippians 2: 9-10 (NIV) says, 'Therefore God exalted him to the highest place and gave him the name that is above every name, that at the name of Jesus every knee should bow, in heaven and on earth and under the earth.'

Humility gives us rest

Have you have been struggling with doing things in your own strength, trying very hard yet with little results from your efforts? Are you intimidated by certain aspects of ministry, struggling to forgive, struggling with relationships, struggling from all that effort? Jesus says in Matthew 11:28-30 (NKJV), 'Come to Me, all you who labour and are heavy laden, and I will give you rest. Take My yoke upon you and learn from Me, for I am gentle and lowly in heart, and you will find rest for your souls. For My yoke is easy and My burden is light.'

Jesus shared His secret here in verse 29 – He tells us that He is gentle, meek and lowly. The same verse goes on to say, 'then you will find rest for your souls'. Rest is when you no longer worry about what others will think or say, when you are no longer afraid of failure. Jesus could rest because of His humility. Jesus had rest because He never did His own thing, He always let the Father do what He wanted to do through Him. Rest is when you no longer worry that something is too scary or too big for you to undertake. Rest is when the thought of what people might think or say no longer has the power to stop you. Rest is when you no longer worry about the outcome when you pray for the sick because you can rest secure in the knowledge that God is the one doing the healing and not you. Rest makes His yoke easy and His burden light.

Humility shows in how we treat those who can do nothing for us

I read somewhere that the true character of a man is best measured by how he treats those who can do nothing for him. If you really want to know how humble you are then the test of your humility is in how well you treat your employees, the waiter, or the customer service assistant. Your humility is even more evident when you humble yourself before those who are in a lower position than you are. Being gifted and talented often makes it harder to be humble. Don't feel you are so great because of your many abilities, talents, and gifts. You simply have a greater responsibility and debt because, as Luke 12:48 (NKJV) says, 'Everyone to whom much is given, from him much will be required.' Success can also make it hard for us to stay humble. Obedience requires humility. We read in 1 Samuel 15 that at first Saul was small in his own eyes until he won a few battles, then he built a monument to himself and started thinking he was smarter than God. It was all downhill for him after that.

When we look at the story of Abraham and his nephew, Lot, in Genesis 13:5-17, we see that Abraham demonstrated his humility by giving his nephew, Lot, first choice. We then see the reward of humility because he who humbles himself will be exalted. God appeared to Abram once again and spelt out the blessing He had for him.

Trigger His favour

Humility is a favour trigger. It is the humble that get favour from God. Humility also attracts favour from people. Every day there are opportunities to grow in humility. Make a conscious decision to search for opportunities to practice humility. The more senior you are in any setting, the fewer opportunities there are to serve. This means you will have to deliberately seek out humility opportunities. Seek them in the home, in the workplace, and in church. Seek out opportunities to practice being humble especially with people who can do absolutely nothing for you. For me, change came slowly but it did come. I had to hit rock bottom and learn to cry out to Him from the very depths because I had truly come to the end of myself. When the Lord revealed the need and the power of forgiveness, it took my humility to obey and forgive. He gave me the grace to obey Him as I humbled myself and then I saw the results of humility as healing began to flow, both physically and emotionally.

As you continue to humble yourself you will notice your very uncharacteristic responses and reactions in many different situations and marvel at the awesomeness of God. The people closest to you – your family, your leaders, and your work colleagues – will all notice. You become unrecognisable! As you become progressively humbler, you become more caring and sensitive, less prickly, and less inclined to always prove a point, or point out that you are right. You are more ready to be the first to apologise and more gracious in any disagreement.

You are becoming who you were always meant to be as you practice humility. You create an atmosphere where the Holy Spirit is comfortable. The most important outcome is that you can carry more of Him. He can trust you enough to send you to someone who is hurting and know that they will hear Him in your voice and feel Him in your hugs and not you. Humility is the doorway to God's favour and to the anointing. Humility is not a means to an end but a state of being which gives us access to the favour of God. If we want more from Him than just the things the gentiles seek, then the key is to decrease and let Him increase more and more.

Are you ready to be nothing so that He can be all in you?

Then let us pray. *Lord, I want to carry more of You. I put on the cloak of humility and I humble myself under Your mighty hand knowing that in due season You will exalt me. I am willing to say no to myself so that I can fulfil all of my purpose. Help me to decrease so that You can increase in me. I thank You that I increase in favour as I grow in humility. In Jesus' name, Amen.*

PART FIVE
Flying free

CONFORMED
TO HIS IMAGE

Conformed to the image of Christ

The Potter's plan was always that we be conformed to the image of Christ. Romans 8:29 (NKJV) says, 'For whom He foreknew, He also predestined to be conformed to the image of His Son, that He might be the firstborn among many brethren.' You become a true ambassador who is able to represent Him in any arena He places you because you exhibit the same characteristics as Him. You can carry His healing power to the sick and His compassion to the hurting. Others will see Him and not you because self is dead. Galatians 2:20 says, 'I have been crucified with Christ; it is no longer I who live, but Christ lives in me; and the life which I now live in the flesh I live by faith in the Son of God, who loved me and gave Himself for me.' This is the result of being conformed to His image.

The transformation process brings you out in your truest form, which is conformed to the image of Christ. It will always involve some pain and challenge, but we will always emerge as an entirely new creation. There are seasons of growing and changing from the inside out, when it looks like nothing is happening and yet so much is going on inside us. We are shedding off the parts that belong to the old man and putting on the new man. In short, we are becoming a new creature.

The caterpillar was always a butterfly even though it hardly looks or acts like one. It has to go through the challenging process of metamorphosis, every part of the process is pretty intense and even lonely because no one except the caterpillar can move through the different stages of immaturity to maturity in order to become what it was born to be.

We admire butterflies when we see them, flying from flower to flower in their beautiful, unique and colourful markings. Perhaps now whenever you see one, take a moment to think about the process it underwent in order to fly freely and pollinate flowers as it does so.

Stay on the wheel

Isaiah 64:8 (NKJV) says, 'We are the clay, and You our potter; And all we are the work of Your hand.' He is the Potter and we are the clay. The Potter has a design and a purpose for the clay. Vessels must be useful. It is not enough for a vessel to be available; it must also be useable. We must be useful in the Kingdom and useful to the Master. Because the Potter has a design and a plan in His mind for the clay, His eyes and His hands are always on the clay. Certain qualities in the clay may render it marred while on the wheel. When He finds anything in us that makes us marred, He doesn't discard us. The Potter doesn't discard the clay because He knows there's nothing intrinsically wrong with it. Instead, the Potter chooses to painstakingly reform us as He sees fit. He knows that things may have happened to the clay while it was on the wheel, so He remakes it into another vessel. Our loving Father never discards us – He simply remakes us. The Potter's name is excellent and He doesn't make shoddy goods. He will do whatever it takes to produce an excellent vessel because we are created in His image. We become transformed as we stay on the Potter's wheel. The Potter knows what He is making, and it is not for the clay to tell the Potter what to make. Our task is to stay on the wheel and not try to wriggle out of the Potter's hands when it gets uncomfortable.

Stay in the Word

Clay needs water to remain soft. When clay is dry, it gets hardened and cannot be reformed. Staying in the Word keeps us soft and malleable. Ephesians 5:26 (NKJV) says, 'That He might sanctify and cleanse her with the washing of water by the word.' Our Father, the Potter, is making something beautiful and useful to the Kingdom so that lives will be impacted. Since we are the clay, we must always remain malleable and pliable in His hands. Any impurities in the clay are removed by the washing of the water of the Word. It is the water of the Word that washes and sanctifies us, so let it work in you. Just as we have a shower or bath daily in order to clean our bodies, so also God uses His Word to clean us on the inside. Hebrews 4:12 (NKJV) says, 'For the word of God is living and powerful, and sharper than any two-edged sword, piercing even to the division of soul and spirit, and of joints and marrow, and is a discerner of the thoughts and intents of the heart.' There are things in our minds, in our character, and attitudes that require cleansing. As we stay in the Word of God, it brings conviction and correction to us. The Word cleanses our thoughts and our motives as we meditate on it and obey it.

Stay in His presence

When we are in His presence our focus is on Him. It is those who remain in His presence who get to live under the shadow of the Almighty (Psalm 91:1). We must stay in His presence because we need strength which comes from joy. Nehemiah 8:10 (NKJV) says, 'For the joy of the Lord is your strength.' We must stay in His presence because joy comes from His presence. In Psalm 16:11 (NKJV) we are told, 'In Your presence is fullness of joy; At Your right hand are pleasures forevermore.' Staying in His presence keeps us attached to the mains as our source instead of being attached to a tank as our source. Times of refreshing come from His presence. We need to be in His presence especially when we feel things aren't working out as planned. We must go there to pour our hearts before Him. We see many times in the Book of Psalms that David would pour out all his problems before God and he would change from complaining about his circumstances to proclaiming God's goodness. Just being in God's presence causes us to switch our focus from our circumstances to Him. Our focus should be on God's ability and integrity. We become full of joy since we know that through Him, we have all the strength we need to accomplish anything. The joy of the Lord is derived from within and is not dependent on external events to sustain it. The joy of the Lord is our strength because it is based on the true unchangeable nature of our God and not on the absence of hardship or pain. Joy remains regardless of the happenings around us.

Get God's perspective

We need the perspective of the omnipotent, omniscient, omnipresent God and not our limited one in order to navigate our way through life successfully. It is when we can look at our lives from His perspective that we begin to recognise that, through the challenges we face, the Potter is remoulding us into a vessel He can use. Ephesians 2:10 (NKJV) says, 'For we are His workmanship created in Christ Jesus unto good works which God prepared beforehand that we should walk in them.' The Potter is sovereign and can turn us into whatever vessel He chooses. We must ask the Lord for His perspective whenever we are facing a challenging situation because His is the right perspective. By obtaining His perspective, we are able to look beyond our immediate discomfort because we have greater vision and a better understanding of His plans for our lives. May God give us His perspective on our circumstances so that we can have the capacity and the patience to remain on the wheel.

The Potter had a plan which He had prepared beforehand when He created you in Christ Jesus; He longs for you to walk in that plan. Jeremiah 1:5 (NKJV) says, 'Before I formed you in the womb, I knew you, before you were born, I sanctified you; I ordained you a prophet to the nations.' He knew you before you were formed in your mother's womb. You are His work of art. As you stay on the wheel, you become who you are meant to be and you line up with the unique blueprint God has for your life. Instead of having your own plans for your life and service to God, you align with His plans for your life and service to Him. In short, you become a vessel worthy of the Master's use. Jeremiah 29:11 (NIV) says, 'For I know the plans that I have for you plans to prosper you and not to harm you, to give you a hope and a future.'

Will you stay on the wheel?

The process of transformation is an ongoing process. We are always a work in progress because God takes us from one degree of glory to the next. If you are feeling like you've been on the wheel for what feels like forever, I want to encourage you to stay on the wheel no matter what. God is faithful, even when we are not or when we feel like giving up. His promises are yes and amen. As we let Him change us by staying soft and malleable instead of stiff and rigid, we can reflect more and more of Him.

My final questions to you as you finish reading are: How much of you is left? How much of "I want", "I think",

"I feel" is left? What are you still not willing to lay down if God was to ask you? When you have to make a choice, is God's way your priority or is it your way?

Just as the caterpillar's journey to its freedom as a butterfly is no walk in the park, our journey of transformation and being conformed into the image of Christ is not without challenge and pain. The journey of dying to self is not an easy process but it is so well worth it.

We start off as a crawling creature, vulnerable to whatever life on the ground throws. As we surrender to being transformed, we emerge as a beautiful new creature living on a higher plane – free, useful, and bringing joy to our Lord and to others.

Make the upgrade from crawling to flying because your destiny beckons.

THE END

Milton Keynes UK
Ingram Content Group UK Ltd.
UKHW012235030923
428004UK00001B/1